THE WORKING PARENT EQUATION

Balancing SMALL HUMANS and BIG CAREERS

I0220729

GEORGIE RUDD

First published in Great Britain by Practical Inspiration Publishing, 2026

© Georgie Rudd, 2026

The moral rights of the author have been asserted.

ISBN 9781788608732 (paperback)
9781788608725 (hardback)
9781788608749 (ebook)

All rights reserved. This book, or any portion thereof, may not be reproduced without the express written permission of the publisher.

Every effort has been made to trace copyright holders and to obtain their permission for the use of copyright material. The publisher apologizes for any errors or omissions and would be grateful if notified of any corrections that should be incorporated in future reprints or editions of this book.

EU GPSR representative: LOGOS EUROPE, 9 rue Nicolas Poussin, LA ROCHELLE 17000, France Contact@logoseurope.eu

Want to bulk-buy copies of this book for your team and colleagues? We can customize the content and co-brand *The Working Parent Equation* to suit your business's needs.

Please email info@practicalinspiration.com for more details.

Endorsements for *The Working Parent Equation: Balancing small humans and big careers*

Positive and empowering: a welcome reminder that being a parent is an asset, not a detractor. I am delighted that Georgie's sage advice has been written down to share with an audience broader than those she can personally coach. Georgie has curated a rich collection of insights and strategies designed to uplift and support working parents. Her warmth, empathy and optimism shine through as she encourages us to recognize the value of parenting skills in the workplace, prioritize those who matter most and extend kindness to ourselves. It's a book I'll revisit whenever new challenges emerge.

Lynn Beattie
Director of Technology, B&Q

An essential read for anyone who's at a point in life where they're wanting to be a brilliant parent AND carry on enjoying a stretching career. It's a challenge that can sometimes feel insurmountable, but Georgie's combination of genuine insight, real-life examples and practical tools makes it a winning read.

Andrew Hill
Head of Marketing, Marks and Spencer

Georgie has written the book working parents desperately need. She refuses to simplify what is genuinely complex, yet makes sophisticated frameworks feel immediately accessible and actionable. Having experienced her approach, I know these tools work. They shift thinking patterns, clarify priorities and create the breathing room we all crave. This isn't about guilt or perfection; it's about sustainable success on your own terms. Georgie combines intellectual rigour with profound compassion, offering both challenge and support exactly when you need it. This is the clear-eyed, honest guide every working parent deserves.

David Harris

Partner and Head of Banking, Baringa Partners

What a great book! Full of so many intensely practical ideas rooted in experience, neuroscience and evidence. With activities throughout, plus an easily accessible structure, this book is designed for the busy working parent who really needs the help it contains. Georgie has offered this book to the world vulnerably, pragmatically and so usefully that I know everyone who needs it will be able to access the stories and support within. What I particularly enjoy in this book are all the stories. There are so many different voices that whoever you are and whatever your circumstances, you will feel reassured that you are not alone, that you are not crazy to want it all, or to struggle to maintain balance, or to work part time and be successful, or to want to take time out for yourself. Thank you, Georgie, for the gentle clarity that you offer working parents. This book truly is a gift for all parents returning to work, and indeed their managers too.

Michelle Parry-Slater

Director of Kairos Modern Learning and Author of *The Learning and Development Handbook: A Learning Practitioner's Toolkit*

I wish this book had been around when I had a young child, and was working and aspiring to achieve success in the workplace. I would have found the guidance, compassion and exercises to be of huge support and nourishment at a time when I was struggling with guilt and a loud inner critic! This book is written with the time-pressured, overwhelmed working parent in mind – it is accessible and very readable (even when exhausted). The writing is underpinned with wisdom and knowledge, drawing on other relevant writers. Each chapter is peppered with short, practical and useful exercises to help reframe thinking and work towards self-acceptance, with supportive 'chapter nuggets' at the end of each chapter to bring the distracted and tired reader back to the salient points. The writing is brought to life through the case studies and quotes from working parents. This book is a must-read for any parent juggling children, home life and career. It is also helpful for coaches who are working with returning and working parents. Although my son is now 23, I am now juggling looking after an elderly mother and many of the exercises have relevance to this context as well. A beautifully written book drawing on Georgie's wisdom, knowledge and experience as a parent of young children and as an executive coach.

Dr Julia Carden PhD, MSc, PCC, FCIPD
Leadership Coach, Coaching Supervisor, Visiting Tutor at Henley Business School and Author of *You Are Not as Self-Aware as You Think You Are*

A must-read for every working parent. *The Working Parent Equation* is a powerful and relatable book that truly resonated with me. Packed with authentic examples and the author's lived experiences, it offers a refreshing blend of insight and empathy. What sets it apart are the practical, hands-on activities that help readers reflect on and recalibrate their work-life balance in meaningful ways. As I turned each page, I found myself nodding and thinking, 'Yes! That's exactly what we face every day as a family.' This book doesn't just speak to working parents, it understands them. It's a thoughtful resource that will help every parent trying to navigate the daily juggle of work and life.

Peter Burnham
Chartered Psychologist, Head of Talent,
Leadership and Performance, Mitie

This is the book I will gift to all my friends as they return to work after becoming parents. Georgie was my return-to-work coach and truly brilliant – supportive, practical and full of wisdom. This book captures her unique approach perfectly, offering the same thoughtful guidance in your pocket whenever you need it. It's like having Georgie by your side, helping you navigate the challenge of combining a fulfilling career and the family you adore with clarity and confidence. I found the lessons invaluable when returning to work after my first maternity leave, and I'm already turning to them again as I prepare for my second!

Caitlin Fields
Customer Director, Baringa Partners

A book I wish I'd read 8 years ago! Goodness how my approach to returning to work (and going on maternity leave in the first place) might have been different if I had only had the chance to meet and be coached by Georgie. Luckily for any future readers, I feel this book is just like talking to her! Georgie's calm, intentional and warm coaching style can be felt from the first chapter. The supportive and inclusive tone of this book will give people the confidence to challenge stereotypes and the space to work out what sort of parent they want to be. In a crowded market of opinions and ideas, this book speaks to those of us who want to be ambitious both in business and at home. I love the exercises – they give space to think and reflect and yet are succinct enough to leave time to make dinner too!

Clare Thornton
Talent Partner, Corporate

What a wonderful, wise and heartfelt book – and finally one that authentically speaks to all working parents, even working dads. Georgie's empathy, passion and practical coaching approach flows off the page, and the warmth and encouraging insights make this a must-read for anyone feeling overwhelmed by the sometimes joyful, sometimes stressful and nearly always challenging family and career juggle. I highly recommend this book to any working parent – packed full of wisdom and applicable ways to balance and thrive within your own unique working parent equation.

Dom Birkby
Head of Transformation, HR Operations & Technology
at a large UK bank

This book is brilliant. Put simply, Georgie gets it. She offers practicality, empathy and wisdom in an easy-to-digest guide for all working parents. She avoids reverting to hacks and silver bullets that won't work for everyone because this is a very personal equation. Instead, this book equips us with relevant ways to get to the most effective thinking we are capable of, especially when we are short on time and under pressure. You'll also love hearing the many voices of other working parents who are navigating similar challenges. If you can't have coaching with Georgie, this book is a close second.

Louise Justham
VP PlayStation Store, Sony

Table of contents

Part 3: Prioritization for professionals

Part 4: Choosing who to listen to

Part 5: Getting unstuck

Part 6: Pulling it all together

Foreword

Finally, a book that offers working parents a unique combination of relatability, empathy and practicality.

When I found myself doing my mascara on the train, debating if there was time to eat lunch and questioning if washing my hair was an achievable goal I wondered: 'When did my working parent equation get so skewed?'

Starting a social enterprise from scratch with a baby and a toddler was a stretch and continues to be a challenge as both my children and the business grow. The work is meaningful and my family is precious.

I know I'm not alone in the daily juggle between ambition, care and identity. Between showing up for others and remembering who we are ourselves.

Georgie Rudd's *The Working Parent Equation* is not a lofty manifesto, it's a practical, compassionate workbook for real life. It's full of tools you can use, even between nursery drop-offs and board meetings, helping us rethink not just how we manage time, but how we define success. Georgie has generously put her wisdom, coaching expertise and care into the hands of every working parent, wherever they may be.

What I love most about this book is its ripple effect. As we balance our own equations, we contribute to something far bigger: a shift in how society values caregiving, equality and sustainability. Every small step we take to look after ourselves, to set boundaries, or to be role models creating workplaces that work for parents, brings us closer to achieving UN Sustainable Development Goal 5: Gender Equality.

This book offers a quadruple win: for ourselves, for our families, for the organizations we lead and for the wider world. Because when working parents thrive, not just survive, everyone benefits.

Cecilia Crossley
Founder, Uplifting People[1]

[1] Author's note: Uplifting People is an amazing community of HR Changemakers. It shares tools and ideas that positively impact people in organizations and beyond. 100% of the profit empowers vulnerable children to be safe, loved and learning – over $1m so far.

Introduction

Welcome to *The Working Parent Equation*. Firstly, let me acknowledge it's taken you some effort to get here. You've created a precious window of time to open this book when time is a scarce commodity as you try to balance the competing demands of your small (or maybe not-so-small) humans and big careers. You may be here looking for an answer to how to balance the equation, you may be in it purely for the practical tools that will make a real difference, or you may be seeking reassurance that you're not the only one who finds this hard. I hope you find all these things here.

In this book we'll be changing the way you think. By combining simple and powerful activities from the world of executive coaching with real-life stories and application, you will have what you need to try things out immediately for yourself. This book is punctuated with simple activities to help you reflect and find new ways forward. Simultaneously, my hope is that you feel folded into the supportive embrace of fellow professional working parents who admit they are a work in progress and are prepared to tell it like it is. You are definitely not alone. In fact, you are in the very best of company.

Who will we be hearing from in this book?

As many different working parents as possible. The stories, examples and contributions are from a wide group of professionals, all of whom I have coached and interviewed. There will be plenty of working Mums' voices in this book; there is much to share and learn. But this is not a book only for working mothers.

It is a fact that fewer fathers take significant parental leave or hold equal or primary responsibility for childcare as I write this, which means there are fewer Dads feeling the impact of the full range of aspects of balancing the working parent equation. However, things are changing for the better: the crucial role for Dads in sharing parental and domestic responsibilities and building relationships with their children is being recognized. Employers are beginning to make steps forward with policies and attitudes to match. It's not within the remit of this book to explore the systemic complexities of this important topic. But what we are going to do is to ensure that we include working Dads in our discussions and hear their experiences, especially those who are balancing the equation by taking a 50:50 or greater share in parenting and domestic responsibilities. We have much to learn from these as yet untapped voices.

We will hear from working parents in various family formations. These are all real people with real things going on. They all want to find ways to be more effective and feel happier. They all want to make the journey a more sustainable one. They have been learning along the way, just like you. All the activities and resources are useful in a practical sense to everyone, regardless of gender and role.

If you are a parent-to-be, welcome and kudos to you for being brave enough to look ahead. I'm conscious that hearing what's coming is a little bit like hearing birth stories before you've given birth: off-putting and informative all at once! My hope is it will help you do some early thinking about what this may all mean for you as a working parent and that you will also feel inspired hearing from others who are walking this path slightly ahead of you.

Managers, welcome. You are one of the most significant influences on how the working parents in your team feel, perform and engage. Many of you are simultaneously a manager and a parent, with insight and understanding that lends you a head-start on how to help other working parents bring their best to work. This book also resources you in managing your own equation to show up at work as the manager you want to be.

And a word for those who are raising your partner's children and/or supporting a partner who is a parent. There is another book waiting to be written dedicated to the particular equation stepparents navigate. The tools are equally relevant to you regaining your own sense of balance and supporting your partner to do the same.

Even more importantly than hearing from others, in this book you will be hearing from you. When you clear away the noise of the outside world and quieten the volume of your own inner monologue, you will notice and hear, maybe for the first time, things that help you rebalance your equation. Tuning into what success looks like for you and learning how to get the best from your own thinking is easier when you can turn down some of this noise.

Where will we be going in this book?

We will explore how you can redefine success in a way that matters to you for the long term; sustainability is the name of the game. We will examine guilt, the mental load and discover a really useful triangle. We will review prioritization, non-negotiables, the 'yes and no' coin and much more. We will acknowledge the voices around us and inside us that throw us off course, finding ways to get an alternative and more useful perspective. And we will look at ways for you to resource yourself for success, as you see it.

When the to-do list is as long as your arm, your brain is about to explode with the sheer enormity of it all and your heart is strung out with the emotional toll, we need new strategies to get a handle on three important factors in the equation: work, family and you. In all likelihood 'you' may have disappeared from the equation.

Where is my Milky Way?

Let me share this to-do list penned by my then 7-year-old which I found on the kitchen table one December. I admit it is a sad indictment of my penchant for a list that my daughter had written one of her own at this tender age. However, it stopped me in my tracks.

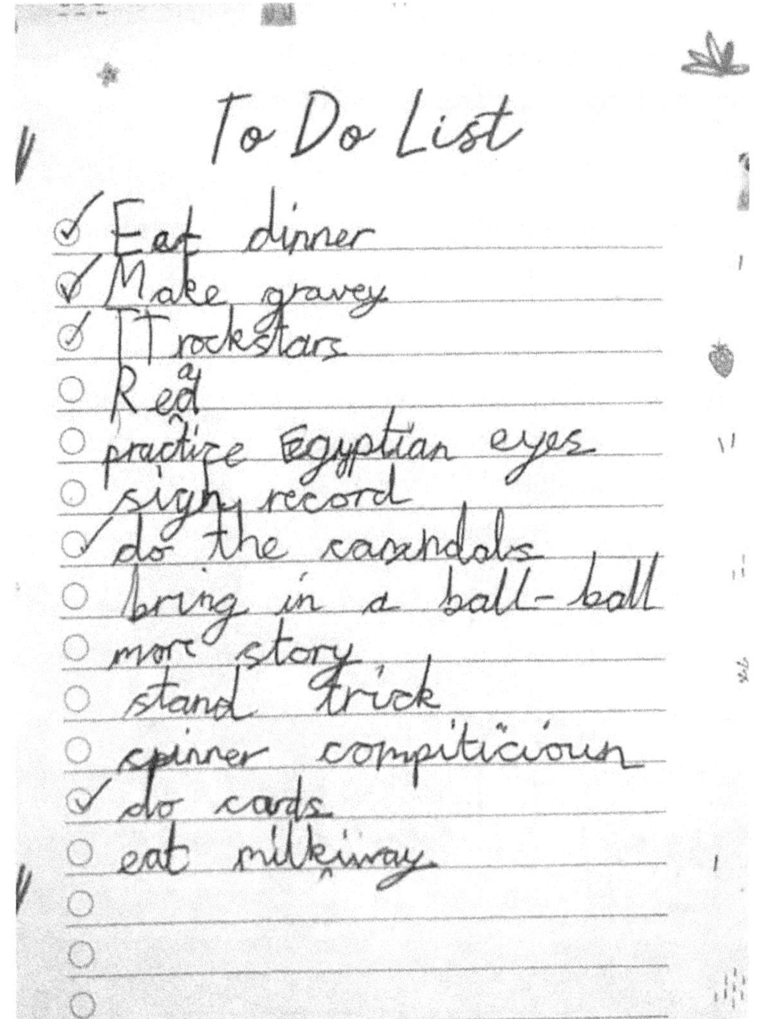

I've included a translation in the footnotes for those who may need it.[2]

[2] Translation of 'to-do' list:

- Eat dinner
- Make gravy (a job she enjoyed, not child labour!)
- TT Rockstars (an online maths times-tables game)

It's an eclectic list by anyone's standards. Unquestionably, she had pressing business to attend to that evening. The final item made me smile. Then I thought to myself:

'Where is the Milky Way on my to do list?'

Where were the things I might want and need to spend time on that would help me balance the equation and run a more sustainable and enjoyable race? What about my relationship with my husband? Where did friendships feature? What about my health? What needed to shift in my priorities? What needed to be demoted to the 'to-don't' list in order to have my metaphorical Milky Way and eat it?

- Read
- Practise Egyptian eyes (make-up for Ancient Egyptian day at school)
- Sign the reading record for school
- Do the candles (light the Christmas candles on our table)
- Bring in a bauble (for the school Christmas tree)
- More story (she was writing a story about a Labrador called Bruce)
- Stand trick (actually I am not sure what that was but it sounds impressive)
- Spinner competition (a science experiment to create a paper spinner and see how long it takes to spin to the ground)
- Do cards (write Christmas cards to her friends at school)
- Eat Milky Way (a small chocolate treat bar)

My daughter had the right idea. Priorities needed to be reviewed and written into the schedule if the Milky Way was to get any focus, and not find itself at the bottom of the list.

How do we balance the equation?

Working parenthood is a finely balanced equation. Our starting point is the recognition and acknowledgement that the working parent equation does not look the same for everyone and there is no one solution. It is complex with multiple variables and is constantly evolving over time as our children grow and our circumstances change. We are adding, subtracting and multiplying continuously and let's not get started yet on what we are dividing. There is no silver bullet because our priorities, values, personal circumstances, emotions, logistics, children, families and more are all going to be different.

And yet, whilst it's a very personal equation these collective things are also true:

- Everyone I know finds balancing small humans and big careers difficult.
- There are common challenges that we all navigate along the way.
- A significant part of how we manage the challenges is deeply connected to how we think about things, how clearly we see things, how well we know ourselves, who we choose to listen to and how well we are resourced.

This book is designed to help people who work in demanding jobs, who feel squeezed by the pressures of their career and family life. Big jobs require big commitment. We are not going to change your work system here in this book and you may not want us to. Work will take as much of you as you are prepared to give it and then some. And your family wants all of you as well. Without diminishing the gift of family, might I suggest you sometimes feel like you are between a rock and hard place? Where is the space? If you let them, both of these priorities will roll in and swallow you whole. And to our earlier point, what about you?

I have discovered through coaching hundreds of professionals that you have the opportunity to create greater clarity and more margin for yourself as the multiple demands roll in. We are more in control than we realize. It is possible to hold back the big boulders rolling towards us and create crucial space for ourselves when we access the kind of high-quality thinking and practical tools that make different choices and decisions possible.

We all want to be great at work, great at home and to feel great. I don't buy into the myth of 'having it all': where in our lives is this ever true? It's always a series of trade-offs, compromises and priorities. A shift from having it all to having what's really important seems much more rooted in reality. I firmly believe that we can make more of our immense capacity to think and make different decisions regarding which part of the equation needs focus, and when to switch it around, so that we can enjoy fulfilment in the round. Undoubtedly, there are really good reasons why we are operating as we are right now and our intent is good. But what if we accessed more liberated thinking that opened up new ways of going about this? What if balancing the equation doesn't mean you getting squashed dangerously out of shape by the big boulders?

Whether we are new parents, seasoned parents, mothers, fathers, parenting couples, co-parents or solo parents, there are times when we need that critical friend to question our perceptions and assumptions and offer the kind of challenge and support that makes us think differently. This book aims to be just that.

Working parenthood is full of joy, humour, delight and discovery. It is also one of the most unpredictable, difficult and stressful pathways we walk as we strive to tread a delicate balance between fulfilling our ambitions at work, being the parent we want to be, the partner we want to be and holding onto the person we wish to be.

None of us can be or should aim to be perfect. Most of us are doing our best, finding our way, making mistakes and learning all the time. What will it take for us to be able to say, with feeling, that we are 'good enough'?

What if you had the knowledge, encouragement and tools to create a clearer way forward?

Let's dive in and find out.

A note on how to use this book

As working parents, at some points you wonder if you will ever be able to concentrate meaningfully on something for longer than you might peruse a menu. My hope is that this book is easy to read, digestible and practical. It is designed to be picked up and put down in short bursts and to be easy to continue with from where you left off.

The sections build on one another in a cumulative way so that you can apply the ideas broadly to working parenthood, and we will develop a kind of shorthand language along the way; it is therefore worth reading the book in order. However, each chapter is a coherent stand-alone unit, so weaving around is an option if that's what you prefer.

In *The Working Parent Equation*, there will be real stories from real people in every chapter to bring things to life, and part of what this book offers is camaraderie. My coaching clients have kindly given their permission to share real examples; where requested, names have been changed for anonymity. Likewise for interviewees who have generously shared their experiences or been quoted.

We never go too long in a chapter before getting to practical activities for you to try out. I invite you to approach this book as a companion and read it in manageable chunks which allow enough time, in one sitting, to get some pen and paper out and try a couple of the activities, most of which are 5–10 minutes in length.

I encourage you to seize the moment and maximize the effectiveness of your attention by experimenting with the activities as you go along, rather than skipping ahead and promising yourself you will come back later. We both know how that will go! If you fancy having everything in one place to capture your responses as you work through the activities, you can download the accompanying workbook at www.ruddcoaching.co.uk. All of the activities are set out with space for your reflections. You will also find a 'quick tools' guide in Chapter 14, listing each activity aligned to 5 key principles, which will take you quickly to something that helps.

Most of all, enjoy having some time to yourself when you're reading the book. It may not be for long stretches at a time but each time you pick it up, *The Working Parent Equation* has your back. Whenever you need to access a balanced perspective, gain a shot of wisdom, find helpful counsel or hear friendly voices who understand the challenge of balancing small humans with big careers, this book is here for you.

Part 1

Redefining success

'I have a bike at home that I use to race other cyclists in a virtual environment. I enjoy racing other people and it is satisfying to beat them but what drives me most is the goal of beating my own time from last session. I'm effectively racing myself.

I've come to realize the same is true but in a less helpful way for my life before and after children. I realize I have been racing my old self (my pre-kids self) and expecting my post-kids self to match or beat that.

But the thing is, the race is different now. Success looks different for me now. I've been racing myself but it's not the same race.'

(Partner, Management Consulting)

1

A different era: From BC to AC

Regardless of when you made the transition from Before Children (BC) to After Children (AC), it is important to pause and reflect. This chapter is as relevant to those of us who are a few years into working parenthood as it is to newer parents. Emma, a Mum of two and Director of Marketing, nearly skipped over Chapter 1 and reflected:

> *'This is so relevant to me even though my first return to work was nearly 10 years ago.'*

Can I therefore invite you to join us?

Big plans

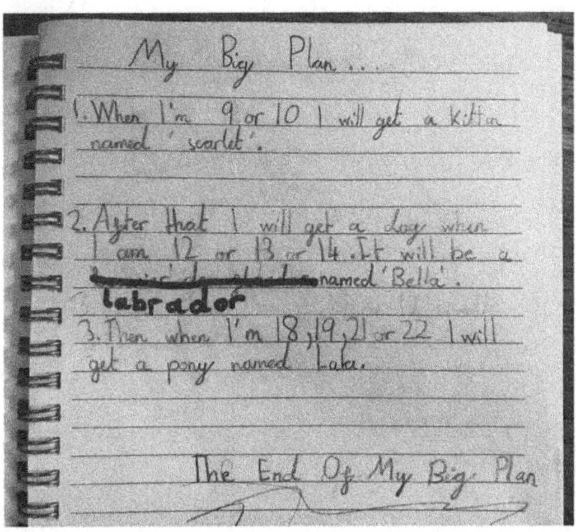

Life is relatively simple when you are 8 years old. This 'Big Plan' is commendable in its aspiration, laser-like focus and notably phased approach to scaling up. It does leave one wondering what exactly is going to happen at the age of 20 that will make having a pony that year an impossibility, whilst 19 and 21 seem to be compatible with pony ownership but, nevertheless, it's clear on success.

We all have ambitions and plans, perhaps not as definitive as 'My Big Plan'. It's rare that our initial plan looks the same as the one we arrive at later, and our vision of success evolves over time. One of the most significant milestones and simultaneous curve balls in our personal journey towards 'success' can be becoming parents.

What got you here won't get you there... sane

It's an understatement to acknowledge that things change when we have children. I love the Marshall Goldsmith[3] line above ('sane' is my tiny addition) which succinctly conveys that as we progress in our lives and our careers, the way we go about creating success needs to evolve. What got us to this point and served us well does not necessarily guarantee success in the new chapter. We will need to stop doing some things, start doing new things and there will be things we need to continue. It is unlikely that we can draw on the same blueprint for every phase; change and growth are essential.

[3] Marshall Goldsmith, *What Got You Here Won't Get You There: How Successful People Become Even More Successful*, 2008.

Goldsmith uses the phrase 'what got you here won't get you there' in relation to leadership transition and development into more senior roles in careers. For working parents, it is equally relevant if we are to enjoy sustainable, fulfilling lives and careers. Our world has expanded and our responsibilities, focus and sources of joy have shifted from the before children era (BC) to the after children era (AC). If we try to continue in exactly the same way as before across every element of our expanded lives, then, amongst other things, burnout shimmers on the horizon. What got us here won't get us there... sane.

One of the first things I hear most frequently in return-to-work coaching is:

'How on earth am I going to do this job now that I have less time?'

Where once we leaned on the lever of time, now we have finite, curtailed windows of time available. First and foremost, we now want to spend quality time with our children and other significant people in our lives. Then we have the practicalities to factor in, such as nursery or school pick-ups, increased family-related social commitments, less available time for a greater load of domestic tasks, child admin, family admin, life admin, the list goes on. Maybe we felt OK pre-children about staying late at work or spending the weekend on work, but now this is not a viable option. We quite simply don't have the time.

What we are prepared to offer to work changes, but also the source of our confidence at work may simultaneously be compromised; for many, confidence has previously been shored up by our readiness to offer our time. When we are unsure of something new or we are dealing with a really challenging project or we have taken on too much in order to demonstrate our commitment, the answer to the problem can often be the hours we put in. As Gail, a senior manager, puts it,

> *'I used to throw time at the issue; I knew I could figure it out and deliver the goods if I put in the hours. Even if I finished late, I could still meet my partner for a late dinner or do a quick gym session and it didn't feel like much of a compromise. I was happy to trade my time for a great result at work.'*

There is a huge logistical shift as we become working parents and there is an accompanying mindset shift as we work out what 'good' looks like now for us, our family and our career. My observation is that it is not uncommon for us as working parents to hold onto the BC blueprint for success longer than is helpful before redefining things for the AC era. Put plainly, if time was an essential way you got things done and built confidence, what now? And when are you going to invest in yourself and your key personal relationships? We need new strategies.

BC success

Achievement is often a key driver, especially for people in big careers. What about you? It will have been a significant part of your success to date, spurring you on to better, ensuring the quality of your work, guaranteeing your commitment and contribution. It has got you where you are.

The concept of success for us as working parents is no less important than before we became parents, but it inevitably looks different in terms of our scope and criteria. Our world, our perspective and the people we care about has expanded. This in turn has an impact on what and how we prioritize and make decisions that align to our version of success for our lives.

Let's take a pause and look back on your BC version of success.

Activity #1: Your BC self

I invite you to indulge in a little time-travel. We are going to step back in time to a version of you before children. Take a moment to visualize yourself.

- What clothes were you wearing?
- Where did you like to socialize?
- Who did you spend your time with?
- How did you relax?

(If this is all too appealing, try to resist the urge to stay there at the end of the activity!)

- Where did you work and who did you work with?
- What was important at work?

OK, now ask yourself the following questions and note down your answers:

a) What did you value most?
b) What did you most want from your career?
c) What did you lean on to create confidence at work?

d) How did you spend your time?
e) What did you give to work from your own time?

Take a look at your answers. What do you notice about your BC self?

Is there a title you could give this BC version of success? (A sort of a headline that you can use as a shorthand to sum up what success was for you.) Write it down.

As an example, one client summarized his BC answers as:

a) Making money and supporting the wider family
b) Fulfilling projects and getting promoted
c) Taking on multiple projects and over-delivering for clients
d) Keeping fit, socializing and working
e) Evenings at work, frequent work travel

His headline was Busy Going Up.

Another parent recalled an image of herself in her office wearing a gorgeous dress and high heels, with immaculate hair and feeling in control. Her title for this image was Polished Perfection, something she feels a long way from now.

What's different in the AC era?

We may still feel aligned to that BC headline whilst we also have new wants and needs as we seek to balance career and family. Being back at work as a parent is different for everyone. We'll dive into the diversity of feelings, thoughts and states of mind in the next section. For now, it is enough to acknowledge that the AC version of success looks different for everyone and that our AC self is different from our BC self.

The quote at the start of Part 1, from a Partner in management consulting, captures this succinctly:

> *'The race is different now. Success looks different for me now. I've been racing myself but it's not the same race.'*

Few of us can fully acknowledge the reality of the seismic shift when we become working parents. Instead, we plough on trying to deliver 100% in every area of our lives and falling foul of this unrealistic bar. We hold ourselves to the BC success criteria we developed, even while we recognize that life has changed so much in this AC era. We may talk about how life is different now and how family is the most important thing, but in performance terms we look in the rear-view mirror at how great we were before at work, get stuck into what's in front of us, focus on surviving, bury the emotions, push hard and wonder if anyone else finds it this hard.

Laura, a director in a consultancy who was close to promotion on her return to work, said this:

> *'I wanted to return at the same level, to be operating at the same high intensity and high-pressure level and I held my own view of what I needed to demonstrate. I told myself I could do it all, even with these new and more important priorities, now I was a mother.'*

Helen, another senior leader, described intense feelings akin to 'grief' as she transitioned back to work after parental leave.

For her, the pre-children legacy of commitment and career success still felt important but the version of herself she knew from before now felt like someone from a previous life: an almost mythical version of her. It took a while to reconnect and that reconnection was shaped differently.

Bernardo Lu-Tsu and his wife emigrated to the UK a few years ago and both work in full-time, demanding jobs. They share childcare and domestic duties 50:50 and have no family in the country. Bernardo Lu-Tsu's definition of success changed after becoming a father:

> *'The meaning of life changed. I want to be successful at work but I now prioritize being there with my son as much as I can. I sometimes feel I am dropping plates at work and it is very frustrating, but I know I am a great Dad and couldn't be there more than I am. Success means accepting things have changed. I'm proud of the way I have been involved.'*

As he says himself, Bernardo Lu-Tsu is 'an exception' when he looks across at his male colleagues at work, because there are not many fathers in his business who have 50% or greater responsibility for the practicalities of child-rearing. We'll come back to this.

Anita, a head of department, puts it this way:

> *'You suddenly know what's really important in your life. No-one can prepare you for how you will feel and how hard it will be. I had a really difficult situation being a single parent almost from the start. I had to work. And I was in no doubt that my daughter was the single most important priority in my life.'*

Rhian, a senior lawyer, took a career break for a number of years to focus exclusively on the equally big job of bringing up her children, and then came back to work later. At that point she wanted:

> *'A role that was interesting, I wanted to be able to earn and I wanted an outlet for my own ambition and not to put all of that into the children. When I noticed I was becoming obsessed about swimming levels for my young daughter I realized it wasn't fair to be holding all that ambition there.'*

Anna, a senior leader in the financial services sector, returned to work with a clear focus on career progression to the next level. She is open about the decision she and her husband took to prioritize her career. Career success for Anna has not changed, but in subtle ways everything has changed:

> *'I didn't get less ambitious but I got more comfortable with a more sustainable route and looking longer-term.'*

She notes that the timing of when she feels ready for the next career step is now less about how quickly she gets to the top but more about when she is ready to invest in that chapter of her career. Crucially, she strongly believes being a parent makes her 'better at work with more perspective'.

Dom, a senior leader in banking, says,

> *'One of my main anxieties before I became a Dad was how I would be a supportive husband, a present, competent and caring father and continue to be effective and high performing at work.'*

A few years on, he now looks at the more senior leaders at work and can't see any that share in the daily care for their children on a 50:50 basis, whether they are male or female:

> *'For my wife and I who are both on promising career tracks, seeing this dynamic above us feels really discombobulating and leaves us with a genuine question about whether it is possible for us to do this differently and both be there 50:50 for our children.'*

Clare, a senior leader in Retail, chose to become a solo parent by donor conception. She reflects that work success is now in sharper relief than before she became a mother as she is:

> *'100% responsible for the financial security of another human being whom I love more than anything'.*

Her focus on work success in the AC era has become higher stakes and of greater importance, not lesser, now that she is a mother, because she is a solo parent. She is going about it differently compared to in the BC era to meet her revised vision of success for her family. For example, she has had to learn to be bold about her boundaries, delegate more and recognize that the time she spends with her son may be a little bit less, but of better quality, than when she tried initially to do everything herself.

Keira became a stepparent to teenaged children when she met her partner. She notes the privilege of playing a role in the children's lives, the joy of a space being created in an existing family system for her, whilst also calling out the complexity of navigating this new role and joining an 'all male tribe' (her partner and his sons). She speaks of the time it takes to work out how to be a blended family and how to stepparent and support her partner in his parenting. There is a lot of grace required in this complicated and sometimes difficult transition to becoming a family.

And you will have your own story to tell. Whilst there are common themes of what every working parent finds hard, each individual has a different experience and feels differently about what they most want at different stages of the journey.

It's important here to also recognize that the journey to parenthood itself plays a significant part: for some, it's been a painful and arduous route of fertility treatment and/or an adoption process with disappointment and heartbreak prior to the joy of becoming a parent. And our experiences during parental leave also shape and change the perspective we return with. For example, Emma's baby was very unwell during the first year of her life and parental leave was characterized by worry, hospital visits and exhausting decision-making.

The nuances of our experiences in reaching this point of 'success' (a child of our own) will shape our attitudes, beliefs, decisions and emotions for AC us. And yet, once we are parents, so many of the challenges of being working parents are common to all; there is an equation to balance no matter how we arrive at parenthood. You can hold incredible gratitude for your precious family whilst acknowledging that balancing the ongoing equation might feel like it is going to break you at times.

Our concept of success and how we define what that is for us has therefore inevitably shifted. Moreover, it is never in a static state. It will continue to need to be revisited as our children grow, we change and the working parent landscape undulates. What got us here won't necessarily get us there again (and repeat).

To set ourselves up for iterative success, we need to start with the end in mind[4] so whatever your stage of parenting, there are important things to pay attention to here. We travelled back in time to the BC era in Activity #1 and now we are going to wind the clock forward to the future to unlock some insights that will inform your AC version of success.

We'll be mining for perspective and a way to explore what is most important to you when we step out of the pressures of the day-to-day balancing act. We're tapping into what you know matters most in your gut and your heart above and beyond what you think in your head.

Activity #2: Meet 80-year-old you

Imagine for a moment that you are able to invite the 80-year-old version of you into the room. As sobering as this may be, spend a minute imaging yourself.

- What are you wearing?
- How does your body feel?
- Where are you?
- Who is around you?
- What are you doing?

[4] Stephen R. Covey, *The 7 Habits of Highly Effective People*, 1989. 'To begin with the end in mind means to start with a clear understanding of your destination. It means to know where you're going so you better understand where you are now and so that the steps you take are always in the right direction' (p. 98).

- What are you feeling about meeting Present You?

Settle in. Reflect on how quickly life has whipped by and what you've learnt about the important stuff along the way. Imagine what it is like not to be working any more.

Now, let's ask Future You a few questions. Try to stay in the mentality of 80-year-old you with all of the above in mind and answer the questions as that version of you. It can help to sit in a different chair from the one you started in: a literal change of perspective.[5]

Write down your answers:

Question to ask Future You	Answer given by Future You
What is really important to you now?	
What is Present You doing well?	
Who do you most want around you at this stage of your life?	
What are you grateful for?	
What do you wish you had done more of?	

[5] There is no clear single originator of the exercise to envisage your future self to access wisdom. Inspirations include Stephen R. Covey, Victor Frankl, Jordan Peterson and Marshall Goldsmith.

What do you wish you had done less of?	
What one piece of advice do you need to give to Present You?	
What small change could Present You make now that Future You will be grateful for?	

What stands out for you as you look at your answers?

Write down or tick your biggest reflections and we will come back to this in Activity #4.

When Otis, a leader in a professional services firm with three primary-aged children, undertook this exercise in coaching he found new insights to help him identify what he really wanted in terms of career progression. He had been wrestling with what success looked like in terms of future seniority, knowing there would be inevitable compromises to make.

When he invited his 80-year-old self into the room and asked him similar questions to the ones in Activity #2, he had laser-like clarity on success. He knew which sacrifices were worthwhile and what he would be most pleased he had spent time on. Rather than some of the big financial plans, restaurants, special trips and a sense of validation from seniority,

'My kids and my wife just want more time with me and I want more time with them.'

What that looked like for him will be different from others; what matters is that he found deeper clarity on what he wanted to be able to look back on and be happy he had prioritized. To an outsider it may sound like a no-brainer; to an individual with all the internal complexity at play, it's a break-through.

4,000 weeks

As Oliver Burkeman puts it in his book, *Four Thousand Weeks: Time Management for Mortals*,[6] we delude ourselves that time stretches on indefinitely. One thing we really do know to be true of our life on Earth is that our time is finite. Burkeman frames this in stark terms: the average life is 4,000 weeks. He notes it is therefore mathematically impossible for us to take up all the opportunities available to us and do all the things we need and want to do (never mind the things we don't want to do) in an average life.

For most of us reading this book, we've already eaten into a fair proportion of those 4,000 weeks. We need to make calls on what we will and won't do, including the good stuff. What may at first seem like a morbid outlook, is a way of understanding how much we are in the driving seat of our lives and how important it is that we don't sleepwalk through. As Burkeman notes, piling on the pressure to live 'a life well-lived' doesn't help; that's another thing to get stressed about! However, modern life has eradicated the value of leisure and just 'being'. Crucially, we've lost the idea of enjoying rest and family time for its own sake rather than for a *reason*. We say

[6] Oliver Burkeman, *Four Thousand Weeks: Time Management for Mortals*, 2022.

to ourselves that it is because we need recovery time from work (implying this is the 'real priority') or because we need to ensure our children grow up as psychologically sound human beings. What about joy? What about being present? How are you approaching your 4,000 weeks?

Activity #3: Stop, start, continue

Reflect on how you are approaching the priorities in your life. Take a look at the following questions and note down your answers.

- What do you need to stop doing?
- What do you need to start doing?
- What do you need to continue doing?

What do you think the small or big shifts need to be for you to run a sustainable race that focuses on what is most important to you?

If we zoom in on work as a starting point, what can you stop, start and continue? Sofia, who returned to work from adoption leave (more on this later), summarized AC changes as follows:

Stop:

- Saying 'yes' to additional projects at work
- Attending so many meetings
- Working at weekends on a regular basis

Start:

- Communicating openly about her schedule and being clear on what she can/cannot take on

- Holding shorter and more focused meetings
- Looking after her physical health

Continue:

- Leaving work early to collect her daughter from nursery and spend this precious time with her
- Prioritizing the development and progression of the work team
- Focusing on commercial results for the firm
- Travelling for work occasionally, albeit on reduced terms

Holistic success and new criteria

We've reflected on differences and shifts between the AC and BC eras for you. What do your AC success criteria need to look like if you are to hold onto what is most important and begin to measure yourself against this?

Let's firstly look at the context. There is a lot in the mix: our own expectations of ourselves and what we ought to be able to achieve, others' expectations of us, societal expectations, the echoes of our family systems, practical realities, the shame associated with pursing career ambitions, the shame associated with not pursing career ambitions. It all adds up to equal a lot more than before for us to manage physically, logistically and emotionally.

Working parents are incredible achievers, often running challenging logistical and emotional marathons before the day really begins. I metaphorically salute fellow parents on the school run as they combine getting children to the right places, dealing with whatever emotional state they find themselves and their children in as they emerge from sleep (or no sleep), multiple last-minute requirements for sports kit, costumes or accessories, client pitches, commutes and a heavy schedule of calls. It is truly amazing what we are capable of. You know what they say, 'if you want something doing, ask a busy person'.

But there is a longer-term issue. We may tell ourselves that it's just 'the juggle' and we are able to cope with it all. Most of us are used to feeling under pressure and are performance-oriented in many aspects of our lives. In fact, some of us would go as far as to say we celebrate the juggle and measure our success on our ability to make it all happen as if it is a badge of honour. But there is a reason so many working parents feel close to burnout, are overwhelmed by the mental load and feel borderline insane at times. Somewhere along the line there is a cost.

More often than not, the cost is you.

Remember those big boulders in our Introduction? Given the chance, those twin demands of work and family will roll right in and there simply isn't space left for you.

So how can you be successful at work, be the parent you want to be and not lose yourself completely along the way?

We need to update the success criteria to what's most important across the holistic picture of work, family and you. How has your personal performance assessment changed? When I work with clients on this redefinition of success, it nearly always begins as a work + family equation in their thinking. It is a surprise when we expand this to be a work + family + *you* equation.

'Oh. I hadn't actually thought about me or what I need in order to be sustainable.'

One of the recurring themes in working parent coaching is how to invest in oneself. The sacrifices most easily made are personal health and relationships. Creating space to be physically active and healthy is key to long-term success. Nurturing our significant relationships needs more intentionality if we are to protect what matters most: partners, relatives and close friends can so easily become collateral damage.

Clarifying the non-negotiables in terms of what we most value and the lines we are not prepared to cross plays a big part. Knowing what your definition of 'being there' for the family is and taking a step back to look at how you are already being successful against your own success criteria helps.

We are not saying careers need to stall or the next promotion has to be deprioritized. It might mean we look at things in chapters; maybe this is a season for maintaining rather than accelerating. How we focus during this 6-month period may not be the same for the next 6 months. Or it may be that we are ready to move forward but in a slightly different mode. Many parents say they have learnt the importance of knowing that things can and will change. When life forces work to slow down, acknowledging there are different chapters is essential to how we manage ourselves through an ever-evolving set of circumstances. Deliberately shifting gears is essential to sustainable success.

Our most brutal critic of our contribution, value and performance is ourselves. There are roles where the organization demands our every waking minute, but there is more within our control than we realize. Is it the firm putting the pressure on you to do 110% or is it you? If you let it, your organization will take as much of you as you are prepared to give; only you can put in the guard rails around your time, energy and focus. The same could be said of your personal version of success at home.

It is a fact that we are now parents. If we don't have a relevant and holistic view of how we are doing across the breadth of our legitimate commitments, the tendency is to look at one area without referencing our performance across the whole. It's typically work that gets the lion's share and we underestimate what we are contributing elsewhere in our lives. When looked at in isolation or through the eyes of our BC self, we will feel that we're not delivering to the same level as we did before. When we look at our total contribution, we access a different perspective.

Activity #4: Work | family | you

Draw three columns. Label them: Work | Family | You.

Work	Family	You

1. Fill in what's really important to you across these three columns.
   Notice there is a column just about you. How are you looking after what is important

to you as an individual so that you can feel better resourced? This 'you' column might include health, fitness, wellbeing, spirituality, friendships and more. Where are you putting the relationship with a significant other if you have one?

2. Look back at what you learnt from 80-year-old you (Activity #2). What does this insight add that helps you prioritize across the areas of work | family | you?
3. Now include a tick against the items where you are already doing well in terms of your priorities. What's working well? If this is hard to do, ask a trusted person to tell you what they see you are prioritizing well.
4. Reflect on the following questions:
   - What do you notice about the columns?
   - Where are your gaps?
   - Where are the elements you have not thought much about before?
   - What does an awareness of 4,000 weeks bring to your thinking?

For Louise, it started small. One step to better 'you' meant eating lunch when working from home. She had got into the habit of giving every minute between nursery runs to work and her own basic needs had fallen off the list.

'My team-mate noticed me eating a bowl of Coco Pops for my lunch online in a meeting and I realized how far from healthy I'd travelled.'

Louise trained full time to be an Olympic-level skier in her BC era so health and nutrition has always been a big part of her life, and yet, she had come a long way from what she knew was important. Her small change to the 'you' column was to add nutritious and easy-to-prepare food for lunch to the online shopping list each week rather than just focusing on getting foods the kids liked. Cooking a bigger evening meal and keeping some leftovers for lunch the next day was another quick win.

Dom describes the importance of marginal gains in the way he and his wife look after themselves. Dom's wife knows she often needs 15 minutes before the day begins to be active, such as taking a short walk. Dom knows he operates better if he gets even 10 minutes of quiet before launching into the morning.

> *'Yesterday, I took 10 minutes for myself before the girls woke up to water the plants in the garden. I was better able to then get the children up, dress them, do breakfast, do the nursery run and arrive for a significant and sensitive meeting at 9am. It's not necessarily about training for an Iron Man.'*

It is easy to get into a whirlwind when our own basic needs have been overlooked. We may not notice it in ourselves or if we do, we justify it with the busyness of our lives. When our success criteria are at the expense of our health, relationships and sustainability, there is huge value in recognizing it and recalibrating.

Finally, one working parent was very committed to their church and decided to add a fourth column to the list given the priority this was. You may also find there is an additional significant priority in your life that deserves its own review.

Nuggets from Chapter 1

- Tap into what 80-year-old you knows is most important to success across the full equation of your life.
- Build new success criteria:
  - What do you need to stop, start and continue doing if your 4,000 weeks are to include enough of the right stuff for you?
  - Widen the lens and look at your total contribution. Review your holistic equation (work + family + you) and notice the current wins, the gaps and commit to one step to better.
- Review this regularly as your children grow, your career unfolds and your personal needs evolve. What needs to be dialled up and down now?
  - Revisit your holistic equation of work | family | you every 6 months.
  - Make a matching coffee date with 80-year-old you to get their view on the above.

2

Why bother trying to balance the equation?

What is it all for?

Even when you know what's most important across your full equation, sometimes you catch yourself wondering if the juggling act is all worth it. Why are you trying so hard to balance the equation when it's costing such a lot? Parenting is a big job in itself; arguably the biggest job of all. When we talk about balancing small humans and big careers, the reality is that we are balancing two big jobs.

I remember driving to school before the train commute with these competing thoughts flitting through my saturated brain. Did I pack my eldest daughter's PE kit and reading record? Did I send that email about the department budget last night? Is the first meeting of the day one that I really need to be at, as I am already running late? Is one of my children showing early signs of anxiety? I *still* haven't booked a doctor's appointment for myself. Will I squeeze through this next iteration of the traffic lights or be stuck here longer?

The clock was ticking rapidly closer to the train deadline and my heart was pumping hard, although the fact I had set the car clock to be 3 minutes fast was always refreshingly helpful. When did 3 minutes become so important? When did 3 minutes signify success versus failure in my life?

Ahead lay a modern workday marathon. Piercing the onslaught of internal ramblings came incisive questions from the back seat about whether I was driving at 30 miles per hour 'like the sign says, Mummy?', 'why do trees lose their leaves in autumn?' and did I know that 'yesterday I did a poo as big as God'?

Standard Thursday.

It is easy to wonder at times why you're putting yourself through all of this, other than, of course, the need to financially support a family and perhaps provide the things you most want your children (and maybe even you) to have in life. Anita, a single Mum, remembers the financial pressure to provide for her family with no support available from her ex-partner. At one point she questioned if it would be better to stop work, given the sky-high cost of childcare, but that would mean giving up on a better future, a career she would enjoy and a sense of validation. A close advisor encouraged her to stick with it through the lean times: 'it may seem pointless now but it will be worth it and good things will come from it'. Anita, now a head of department, reflects that it did bring her a better future. And almost more importantly, when being a single Mum felt lonely and confidence-sapping, her work offered a sense of worth, achievement and optimism that she brought home with her: 'it made me a better Mum'.

What about you? Maybe you question if you need to work at such a senior level, whether you need to work the pattern you do or whether you need to work in the kind of high-pressure environment you find yourself in. Maybe you occasionally wonder if it would be better to step back from it all and prioritize parenting and family over career and job.

Whatever the circumstances, it's key to consider your reasons for doing what you are doing and work out your own perspective on what the findings of this mini-'why'-audit mean for you.

Laura initially felt torn between the value she placed on progressing her career and the value she placed on being a parent. She looked backwards at the decision her own mother had taken to be at home full time and wondered if that was what she was supposed to do.

- Was it 'selfish' to want to progress her career?
- Was it ok to admit that she didn't want to let go of all the years of hard work and commitment when she was so close to her ambition to become a partner in the firm?
- Was it ok to acknowledge that this meant a lot to her?
- Was it ok to say out loud that she wanted her family to have the kind of financial resources, experiences and lifestyle that were not a feature of her own childhood, as happy as it had been?

She concluded it was important and acceptable to want to progress her career; it was a big part of her 'why'.

Tom, a leader in the energy sector, reduced his work pattern to 4 days a week in order to be more present for his children, take on more of the domestic load, give weekends a chance of being better-quality family time and regain a sense of sanity. Colleagues seemed to be mainly supportive but surprised. He talks openly about the sense of judgement he sometimes feels and whether others doubt his commitment as a result of his decision, which occasionally wobbles his 'why'.

Damien stepped back completely from working as a paramedic for a significant period of time when he found himself suddenly solo parenting. There wasn't a choice for him but his 'why' of being there for his children was tested as he battled intense periods of loneliness and feeling like an outsider. As the only Dad at the school gates hoping to create connection with an exclusively female group of non-working parents, he felt isolated. Despite leaning towards extraversion and usually finding it easy to make friends, he couldn't find a way in. It added to a sense of being an oddity and, occasionally, a failure. There are challenges Dads face that are subtly different from Mums.

Understanding and acknowledging what motivates you can often mean making different decisions from others around you or from how things were done in your previous family systems or workplace systems. We shall return to this idea of systems and the hold they have over us. For now, I invite you to spend a few moments having an honest conversation with yourself about your reasons for trying to balance your small humans and big career, especially if the cost feels high. Work is hopefully an area of your life that brings you fulfilment and enjoyment and I am equally hopeful that your family brings you satisfaction and deep joy. But sometimes keeping the entirety of this crazy show on the road leads you to the edges of your capacity to cope.

Permission to know your 'why'

Accepting that the majority of us need to work, it may feel self-indulgent, unnecessary or even shameful to articulate why we want to work in a specific industry, a particular role or adopt a certain work pattern. It may feel pointless to examine whether the equation could look different for you when you feel there is no other way to look at it.

Notice if you feel the rise of a critical voice that whispers in your ear 'you are navel gazing' and instead turn your attention to the idea of effectiveness.

I've found with clients that it is effective to say or write down what is most important to them about why they are working the way they do, why they do what they do and what they most want from work. This is liberating, especially if they secretly doubt the validity of their perspective when it goes against the way they were brought up or the expectations of significant others in their lives. When we are aligned to what we really value, we are more effective in carving out the boundaries, making prioritization decisions and sticking to our non-negotiables. So rather than feeling that this is self-indulgent, can you see that this is strategic and a core element in balancing your own equation in a way that works for you?

Activity #5: Why are you doing this?

Reflect on the sections of the wheel below. If you feel an element is missing or you'd like to replace the categories, feel free to do this.

Consider how important each segment is to you personally, without worrying about what other people might think of your opinion, and mark which point on the scale reflects how important that segment is to you.

1 = of low importance to you

10 = of high importance to you

Once you have placed your markers, join the dots to create a shape on the wheel. You may see some spikes, dips and flat areas.

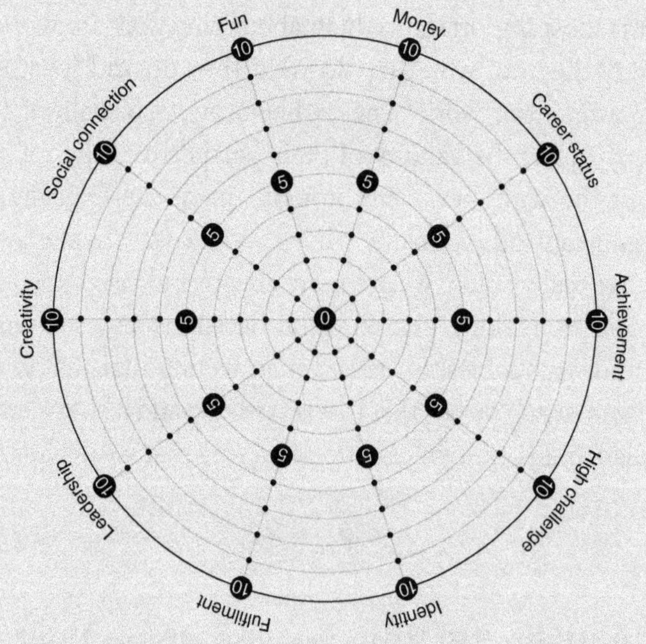

- What do you notice about the shape of your diagram?
- What are the biggest drivers for you?

- Where are the surprises or what had you not articulated clearly to yourself before?
- What does this mean for why you are working the way you do?

Felicity initially felt conflicted about the importance of money and career status in her wheel. She was really motivated by working with great people, belonging to a team and working through challenges. She didn't live for material rewards but it was intricately connected to her 'why'. It was a breakthrough to say out loud that status (reaching the top of her profession) and money (financial security and reward for a complex and demanding job) were of high importance to her. It allowed her to pursue her career ambitions without feeling in conflict with what others might say.

Validity of your 'why'

There are numerous scripts about what we are supposed to prioritize; what society, family and others think we ought to want. It is not difficult to get ensnared in what others tell us is a valid way forward and to doubt ourselves.

For example, sometimes it can be new to honestly acknowledge that creativity is important to you. Or that the scope for intellectual challenge is intrinsic to your 'why' and it doesn't make you a bad parent for wanting that. Or to recognize that getting that promotion to a more senior role is not actually what you want because you wish to expend your energy on different things. Or that you wish to step back from work because it's important to you to be more present for your family than your current work allows.

Let's consider what it is that is telling you that your reasons for balancing the equation are not valid. Maybe a small (or loud) voice is saying 'that's not what people like you are meant to do'. Perhaps you feel someone significant in your life would be displeased with you? It could be that you feel guilt or shame about the way you want to balance work, family and you. It's possible you feel a satisfying sense of rebellion for prioritizing things differently from others in your life but that this rebellion for its own sake is not really what makes you happy.

The important thing is to work out what it looks like when you are in the driving seat and to be able to hear what you really think.

Activity #6: Validating your 'why'

As you reflect on your 'why' wheel, to what extent do you feel your drivers are valid?

- What (or who) might you need to let go of in order for those things to be acceptable reasons for doing what you are doing?
- If you knew your 'why' drivers were valid, what would you change?

Sticky systems

We're going to step further into the realm of understanding previous systems you've belonged to and the idea of letting go of less relevant imperatives.

Systems are essentially 'groups'. You will undoubtedly have belonged to a number throughout your life: your family of origin (the family you grew up in), schools, colleges, sports teams, universities, workplaces, your new family now you are a parent and more. Systems can be pretty sticky, especially when you are trying to validate why you are balancing your equation the way you most want to.[7]

Who are you being loyal to?

We like to think we are unique beings operating independently in our own space with our own direction, values and drivers. We say things like, 'I know my own mind', 'I'm my own person', 'I'm carving my own path' or even 'I've left that all behind me'. Yet we are all naturally part of wider pictures that have shaped and formed us over time and which leave invisible traces as we move on.

Our very first experience of this is in our family of origin. There are behavioural norms, learned expectations, highly prized values, role models demonstrating how to 'be' and multiple formative experiences. As children, our greatest need is to belong, so we are acutely attuned to what we pick up in this original system and it can have a life-long tail. This is a very good thing in so many ways. There is much we learn in our original family system that continues to serve us well, such as integrity, the importance of family, work ethic and so on. But as we move into new systems with different

[7] The originator of family system theory is Burt Hellinger who influenced the work of John Whittington. This exploration of organizational, professional and personal relationship systems is inspired by John Whittington, *Systemic Coaching and Constellations: The Principles, Practices and Application for Individuals, Teams and Groups*, 2016.

norms, expectations and ways to belong, not all the same things remain as relevant. It's similar with work systems.

It may be that some of the things you are struggling to do or make a change to (permission for your 'why' in balancing the equation) are tied into your loyalty to previous systems. We heard earlier that Laura initially felt conflicted as she looked back at the role-modelling in her family of origin on what motherhood was supposed to look like, and wondered if she should be disloyal to that pattern by having a career beyond children. And yet, she was part of a different generation, a different family set-up in a different country and was going in a different direction.

Ethan, a director in a professional services firm, found it hard to prioritize family holiday time because his own parents, who had set up a business as first-generation immigrants, had never taken holidays. Throwaway comments from his parents like 'it's alright for some' took him straight to feeling guilty about doing things differently from his family of origin and there was a cost to his consequent actions within his own new family.

Sometimes, we are tethered by an invisible thread to a previous system dynamic that lasts beyond its usefulness or relevance to our present situation. We can break free with huge love and respect for what went before if we treasure the people and the system. We're not necessarily rejecting it. We are merely working out what is relevant. John Whittington, author of the definitive book on coaching constellations, puts it this way:

> *'To grow and develop we must become guilty in relationship to a previous system.'*[8]

[8] Whittington, *Systemic Coaching & Constellations*, p. 55.

What does this mean for you? Well, for example, if a strong role model in your family demonstrated a ferocious work ethic, you may find it hard to be disloyal to this individual or value by letting yourself rest, even when logic and your body tells you that's the best thing.

If you previously worked in a company where hierarchy was king, you may resist asking more senior people for help on a challenging project for fear of not owning the problem or wasting the time of someone 'important'. And yet, those more senior people can and want to help you.

You may know you want to step back from work but you are held back by the echoey voice of a family member or past boss who would disapprove or, indeed, the opposite scenario.

Until we pinpoint what it is that we gladly take with us from our systems (i.e. what we are grateful for and still serves us well) and identify what we've carried with us that we need to leave back in that previous system, it can be hard to make change.

Petra, a consultant, was aware of her tendency to prioritize work over her own health. If she was sick, she would often push through, logging on from home while she was ill when the more effective option would have been to switch off from work and rest and recover more quickly. In the long term she was prolonging the period she was ill, feeling stressed and was unable to deliver the quality she prided herself on. Additionally, she was holding too much at home as well as at work. She did not feel ok about requesting more child-related support from her husband or work input from her colleagues, even though they would all have been happy to help.

When we explored Petra's family system, it became clear that she was borrowing from the past and trying to keep loyal to that in the present day. She describes her father as driving on with work to the detriment of family, holidays, health and even haircuts. The echoes of his voice would play out for her along the lines of 'if you are not super hard-working, you're not doing well'. It meant Petra didn't stop when she was ill, was slow to ask others for help both at work and at home (feeling she should do it all herself) and was burning through precious reserves of energy.

Petra identified that whilst there were many things she was glad to have learnt from this family system which had helped her to get to where she is today, there were elements that were not as relevant to her life now as a professional, a wife and a mother. The prioritization of work above everything else was her father's imperative, not hers. She needed to leave that behind with him. This may seem obvious but so often we have not stopped to sort out what to take forward and what to leave behind, and it runs so deep we may not even have noticed it before. Petra reflects:

> *'Even if you have not gone all the way in addressing it, just understanding and being able to notice when you are doing that and unpicking that a bit is so helpful.'*

Surfacing the hidden loyalties that are directing your thinking can be revealing. You can decide what you want to thank your systems for and keep for the future. This is a powerful activity to garner all the positive energy and support of those experiences and people and to accelerate with all that goodwill under your wings. You can also decide which people or values or norms you respectfully wish to leave behind and which bear less relevance now or whose issues you don't need to solve. The point is, you don't have to carry everything forward with you. Once you realize this, the route to longer-term change can be much less sticky. It's liberating to cut the invisible ties and rediscover the brilliant strengths that those you've known in your life have fostered in you. Far from pronouncing what is 'right and wrong', it's about what is relevant.

Figuring out what is relevant and what is a hangover from previous systems is not only useful as we consider family units. It is just as powerful and pertinent to our experiences in the working environment.

Henry, a working Dad in change management, was on the cusp of promotion to a very senior level at his firm but both he and the firm were concerned he might burn himself out. He needed to bring more balance to his approach to work and home and ask more senior people to help rather than trying to own all the issues himself. As an engineer, he had previously worked in a manufacturing firm where the company mantra for all managers was 'Be Here Now'. So, if something cropped up on the manufacturing line, managers needed to be there immediately, take accountability and stay until they solved it.

He had left manufacturing behind and joined the world of consulting where there were similarities but also some big differences: senior people expected to be involved, to be asked for input and consulted. Not all issues depended on Henry alone.

When he reframed this in the context of his present system at work and also his family system (a wife and two children), he saw the need to flex 'Be Here Now' to apply more broadly to all his priorities in life: home was a valid place to 'Be Here Now'. He valued much of what his earlier career had taught him and knew it was a big part of his success to date, but it had begun to erode his career progress and happiness. We are back to 'what got you here won't get you there'. It required leaving behind some things that were less relevant to him now; a significant change of perspective more aligned to what was most important now.

Activity #7: Stepping out of a sticky system

Find an empty table and a quiet space. Whilst this may seem nigh-on impossible in your busy home, it is worth doing. Maybe you can make the first work meeting of the day a meeting with yourself and find a room in the office or a space on your home desk to do this? Have a couple of pens and some sticky notes to hand.

There are 9 steps below to work through; taking approximately 15 minutes, it is the longest (but one of the most revealing) activities in the book, so you may need a coffee too.[9]

[9] This exercise is adapted from Whittington, *Systemic Coaching and Constellations*, p. 92.

Step 1

What change are you most struggling to make in your working parent equation?

- Look back at Activity #4 to see what you most want to prioritize across work | family | you.
- Look back at Activity #5 on your 'why' drivers, to see what is important to you but where you feel most conflicted.

Which system might you be being loyal to in your struggle to make a change? It might be a previous workplace, your family, an academic institution etc. If you are not sure, your family of origin always has important information to offer. Choose the system you want to look at.

Step 2

Select a sticky note to represent yourself and write 'Me' on it. If you have different coloured sticky notes, choose a colour that feels right to represent you. Colour is a shorthand to emotion so listen to your gut on what feels right! Place the 'Me' note on the table in front of you where it feels right to place it.

Step 3

Who or what is the next most important sticky note to put on the system map that is, or was, key to that system? It may be parents, siblings, significant adults, a teacher, a significant boss, a sports coach, theatre director… or it could even be certain strong values, rules, behaviours. Write the name of the person or thing on the sticky note and place it on the map in the place that feels right. Think about where it should go. Is it near the 'Me' sticky note, far away from 'Me', to the left or the right, above or below… ?

Step 4

Repeat Step 3 for further significant people or things and place them carefully and thoughtfully on the map in the places that feel right to you. Think about proximity to the 'Me' sticky note and to each other, and think about the direction they are facing (you can draw an arrow on the sticky notes to show which way they are looking if that helps).

Step 5

When you have placed the most significant people or things on the map, lean back. Try not to make it a huge map but stick to the most significant people or things and keep it fairly small. Ask yourself the following questions:

- What do I notice about my place in this system?
- What do I notice about what is close and far away from 'Me'?
- What might it mean for me?

Step 6

Place some further sticky notes on your map next to significant people or things and capture what they are saying or what their beliefs are. For example, Petra's sticky note for her Dad said: 'Work hard; don't take a break'.

Step 7

When you have added the sticky notes on what the people or things in your system are saying or believing, lean back. Ask yourself the following questions:

- Who or what am I paying most attention to?
- Who or what have I not been listening to?
- What am I glad to be carrying forward with me and what is still relevant from this system?
- What would I like to leave behind in this system? It was not mine to begin with or is no longer as relevant to where I am now. (If this feels difficult, imagine you have a bag that you cannot fit everything into. If you had to decide on something to leave behind in order to make space for something you definitely want to take with you, what would stay out of the bag?)

Step 8

Using what you identified in Step 7, say out loud, 'thank you (x) for giving me (y). I am glad to have this with me still and it is still serving me well today. I am grateful to you for this'.

Say out loud, '(x), with love and respect [or whatever feels most appropriate to you], I am leaving (z) behind with you. I don't need to hold onto this so tightly any more; it is not serving me well now. It's yours, not mine'.

Step 9

Give yourself a few minutes to process what you have discovered. It may help to talk to a trusted friend, partner or coach about what you want to take with you and what you want to leave behind.

The next time you notice yourself being loyal to something you chose to leave behind, remember why it is no longer as relevant and what would be different for you if you were no longer loyal to this. Imagine your bag is not big enough to take everything forward; what are you choosing to give space to?

Nuggets from Chapter 2

- Have an honest conversation with yourself about your reasons for balancing career and family. What's driving you? Write it down.
- Take the time to identify the 'why' drivers that mean the most to you and what they bring you: use the Why Wheel to help you.
- What can you acknowledge is important to you that has felt difficult to acknowledge before?
- Look at your systems. Whose voice or whose influence can you hear that may be getting in the way of you reconciling your 'why'?
- Say out loud what are you glad to be carrying with you from a previous system and what can you let go of because it is not as relevant to you now.

Part 2

Game-changing thinking

'If thinking clearly is the thing on which everything else depends, it is dangerous to keep doing the things that stop it.'

(Nancy Kline, *Time to Think*)

3

Balancing the equation through better-quality thinking

How we think is everything. When we are tired, time-poor, stressed and worried, it is very easy to follow well-trodden, less helpful paths of thinking or be knocked off-course by a skewed internal view of what is happening. A big part of balancing the equation of working parenthood is finding ways to access the most balanced thinking we are capable of.

A really useful triangle

Let me introduce you to a simple, yet powerful triangle that helps us remember how big a part thinking plays in our effectiveness. Meet the Cognitive Triangle.[10]

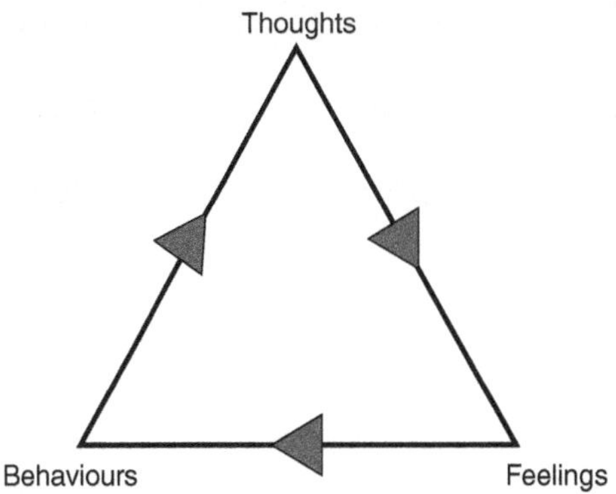

[10] The Cognitive Triangle was devised by psychotherapist Aaron Beck in the 1960s. The Cognitive Triangle and the related Cognitive Triad are used in cognitive behavioural

The basic principle of the triangle is that what we *think* influences how we *feel* and how we *behave*.

We can be tempted to look at how we behave or how we feel in isolation, without necessarily considering the thinking that has led to this feeling. We may just know we feel disappointed or sad or a bit stuck. We may say or do something that we wish we hadn't and feel bad about that, without working through what got us to that point and what might have helped to course correct before we got there.

The first step to better is to examine what we are thinking, as this is something we can change. Instinctively, this makes sense.

Take this small example:

'You walk past someone you know well in the street and they totally ignore you. What are you thinking at that moment? What are the consequences for how you feel and behave?'

Your feelings and how you behave in that moment and the next time you see that person are influenced by the first thought, which may be something along the lines of:

'They deliberately ignored me; they don't want to talk to me.'

You may feel hurt, surprised, upset or puzzled. For some of us, there will be rumination as we continue to wonder why

therapy (CBT). You don't have to read up on this further or go to therapy in order to see the principles that are relevant in the everyday flow of life. Of course, if you are noticing a prevalence of negative thoughts or symptoms of depression or anxiety, this book is not an answer in itself and I encourage you to talk to your doctor in the first instance.

they ignored us and what this might mean. A small moment can lead to emotional energy being expended unnecessarily. Maybe, as a consequence, when you next see them you avoid them or give them a bit of a look, or try extra hard to be friendly to them to ensure you have not upset them.

If the thought was different, how would your feelings and behaviour be different?

The alternative thoughts in this example are, of course, that the person did not notice you, did not have their contact lenses in, was in a world of deep thought, was hurrying, was having a really tough morning, didn't want to talk to anyone. If you realized any of the above it would immediately change how you felt and how you behaved.

Thoughts are powerful. If we can develop ways to think really clearly, we can alter how we feel and behave. What we give our attention to grows.

Alternative thoughts

Sylvie was in the process of reconciling her BC (Before Children) reputation for commitment with the significant change to her working day in the AC (After Children) world of nursery pick-ups. She knew picking up her child from nursery was a necessity and a priority. She and her husband shared the nursery runs across the week evenly. There was no question in Sylvie's mind that leaving to collect her daughter was the right thing to be doing, but it felt so different from the Sylvie who had previously attended late meetings and been the last to leave most nights.

When she left work earlier than the others in the team to do the nursery pick-up, this is what she *thought*:

'Everyone thinks I am not pulling my weight; they think I am a slacker.'

She then noticed the following *feelings*:

Sadness:	'My value to the team is in doubt.'
Guilt:	'I'm letting people down.'
Worry:	'I haven't finished that piece of work.'
Frustration:	'I won't be part of the conversation at the late team meeting.'
Anger:	'Slacker is unfair. I'm running the marathon tonight of nursery pick-up, tea, bathtime, settling the baby, resettling the baby… '

This thinking and feeling prompted the following *behaviours*:

- Sylvie had some intense imaginary conversations in her head that evening with colleagues, where she justified leaving work when she did. It took up a lot of her mental energy.
- She became preoccupied and distracted while she was bathing her little girl and conscious she was rushing story time rather than engaging as fully as she wanted to.
- She snapped at her partner when he arrived home from work.
- She logged back on to her laptop later that evening and worked until late to prove she was not a slacker.
- And, simultaneously, she eroded her recovery time that evening to refresh and reboot for the next day.

Hands up if you recognize Sylvie's story?

If we go back to the thought that sparked all of this, it is of course a possibility that the team thought Sylvie was a 'slacker'. But when she examined the evidence for this, there wasn't much to go on. In fact, she was less sure her departure had even registered, given how focused everyone was. And even if there had been some rumblings, which there hadn't been, she knew she was doing the right thing in her AC definition of success and that outputs counted more than hours.

These alternative and truer thoughts were more helpful to Sylvie:

- 'I will have an opportunity tomorrow to get the 2-minute executive summary of the meeting I missed.'
- 'The thing I am working on is not due immediately.'
- 'My colleagues know I am as passionate about high-quality work as ever.'
- 'I can role-model prioritization to more junior members of the team, especially other working parents.'

Alternative thoughts do lead to alternative feelings and behaviours.

Nancy Kline incisively illuminates the criticality of clear thinking in her book, *Time to Think*:

> *'If thinking clearly is the thing on which everything else depends, it is dangerous to keep doing the things that stop it'.*[11]

We need to be doing our best thinking if we are to behave as effectively as possible. High-quality thinking means we show

[11] Nancy Kline, *Time to Think: Listening to Ignite the Human Mind*, 1999, p. 70.

up the way we most want to. And let's be honest, working parents have so little slack in the system and so many real things to worry about, that we cannot afford to expend mental energy on erroneous thinking.

Activity #8: Rewind the Triangle

Reflect on a time as a working parent that you had a thought that sparked negative feelings or meant you behaved in a way that you later regretted.

Work through the triangle starting at the *thought*. For example, 'I'm letting the team down'.

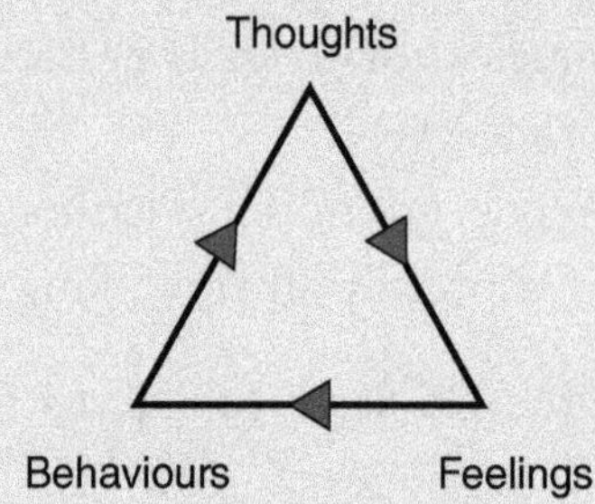

- What was the *thought* that sparked the reaction?
- What *feelings* did you notice?
- What did you *do* as a result?

Now, replace the thought with a new, more helpful thought. What else might be true and more helpful to think than the pejorative assumption?

Work through the Triangle again. If you had the different and more helpful *thought* you identified above:

- What *feelings* would follow?
- What would you *do*?

As you look at your answers, what do you notice would have been different for you if the thought had been different?

Lindsey, a partner in a professional services firm, was due to go on holiday for 1 week in the run-up to Christmas and her family were concerned work would erode this precious time and much-needed recovery. There's no doubt about it, Lindsey has a full-on job. She was aware that the balance had tipped into an unhealthy zone: her dedication to work was having an impact on her family and her health. This was an opportunity to unwind and really connect with their teenaged children.

Lindsey retraced back to the thoughts which were sparking her intention to take the laptop on holiday with her.

> *'If I switch off, I will let my team down and jeopardize the client opportunity. A key client pitch might need to be finalized while I am away and I will need to work on it.'*

Lindsey knew she really needed a break at the end of a long year and so she challenged this thought with alternatives.

What if these thoughts were truer?

- 'The team is senior and capable enough to be able to handle this.'

- 'My colleague can have oversight for me.'
- 'I can comment if absolutely critical without needing my laptop.'
- 'One week's break is reasonable; if I don't get a break I will be less effective.'
- 'I want my family to know and feel how important they are to me.'
- 'My children are growing up and the time for us to be on holiday together is receding as they become increasingly independent.'
- 'Leaving my laptop at home is a signal to myself and my family that this time together is important.'

Lindsey reported having a higher quality break as a result of her decision. We can absolutely see how she got to the point she reached. Tunnel vision is easy to slip into when you're engaged in your work, you care and you are under pressure. It's essentially an overplayed strength. The key is to recognize when the strength has become unhelpful to your holistic success criteria and where dialling it down will enable enjoyment (remember 4,000 weeks) and longer-term, sustainable success.

A scientist, a historian and a journalist: Liberation through evidence testing

How we think and talk to ourselves, who we choose to listen to and what we know to be true about our values and version of success has much more impact than hacks and advice. I firmly believe that learning how we can think better is at the heart of balancing the equation and that sustainable success depends on us maximizing the huge potential of our minds.

We can learn to question the assumptions we are making. Our first thought is not necessarily the best thought or the one that is reflective of how things really are but, as humans, we have learnt to operate on assumption for speed. As working parents there is high cognitive load in a time-poor environment, so the assumptions are necessary in order for us to get on with life. But there is a real benefit in introducing some challenge to the assumptions, especially when we are feeling overwhelmed.

Adam Grant, a professor and author in the field of organizational psychology, encourages us to think like a scientist in his book, *Think Again*. He writes of the power of humility and curiosity over pride and conviction:

> *'Thinking like a scientist involves more than just reacting with an open mind. It means being actively open-minded. It requires searching for reasons why we might be wrong – not for reasons why we must be right – and revising our views based on what we learn.'*[12]

We can question our hypothesis in the face of new evidence and learn more flexible ways of thinking. We can notice the stories we tell ourselves and examine the data we think we have. If science feels at arm's length to you, an alternative

[12] Adam Grant, *Think Again: The Power of Knowing What You Don't Know*, 2021, p. 25.

might be to look at things as a historian might do. We're looking for evidence and corroboration to support a point of view and substantiate what we are assuming. Or if being a journalist appeals more, it's a similar idea. There are two sides (at least) to the story and we're trying to establish what is the most accurate version of the truth; we're mining for the real story.

If we look at our own theories and hypotheses about what we 'must' do, what we 'can't do' or what is possible with more attention to the evidence, we may see things differently or at least feel clearer about the assumptions we have made.

Maddie, a retail leader in the UK, was flying solo for a month while her partner was away on business in Africa. She felt completely overstretched. There was a promotion opportunity at work that she had been considering for a while. As she surveyed the devastation across the living room left by her two young children, ploughed through the long list of tasks and worked out the logistics of the days ahead, she found herself thinking:

'There is no way I can go for promotion with everything else I've got on.'

Her 'can't' in this instance is understandable. Based on the immediate scenario, we can see how she got there.

She channelled her inner historian. It was true that this month was a huge stretch, but what did the broader and longer-term evidence add to the story that facilitated different conclusions?

Historian's perspective	Different conclusion
This period was not the norm. Shifting from two parents to one parent was not reflective of the longitudinal picture.	To base her decision on how she felt right at that moment was to ignore the longer-term possibilities.
She had experienced moments of overwhelm in the past and the intensity of that feeling had always lessened in time.	There were definitely better times she could remember when things felt more in balance than the present.
The temporary nature of the solo full-on juggle meant her childcare support system was not set up to cope with this scenario.	This meant either accepting this was a temporary situation or reviewing the arrangements. Either would enable new ways of coping.
She had not slept much over the last few weeks. Self-care was non-existent.	She could ask friends and family for more help rather than trying to do it all herself. Exhaustion was clouding her view.

What decisions are you grappling with that would benefit from some time with your inner scientist, historian or journalist? Why not invite them in to look at what you think you know and check that it is the whole picture?

Activity #9: Channelling your inner scientist, historian or journalist

Take 5 minutes with a notepad and a pen. Consider a current story or hypothesis that's occupying your thinking.

Write down your answers to the following questions. Remember you're looking at this as a scientist, or historian or journalist to find the truth.

- What is the story you are telling yourself about the current situation?
- What are you feeling about yourself and the current situation?
- How true is what you are thinking? What evidence or data do you have to support or dispute your current thinking?
- What are you assuming?
- What would a good friend say to you at this moment?
- What is more true and helpful to be thinking?

Write a 'for' and 'against' list of data or evidence to support or dispute your hypothesis.

- If you now reframed the story or hypothesis, how would you articulate it?

Nuggets from Chapter 3

- Rewind the Cognitive Triangle: what would be different about how you felt and behaved if the thought at the top of the triangle was different? Ask yourself 'what is more true and helpful than that original thought?'
- Use the Cognitive Triangle once a week to review a thinking distortion you spotted. You could have a discreet triangle diagram reminder on a sticky note near your computer or in your work bag or as a diary reminder in your online calendar.
- Question assumptions about a current hypothesis or story. What would your inner scientist or historian or journalist draw on to support or disprove that?
- Write a 'for and against' list of evidence about what's going on and mine for data to support or dispute what you are saying to yourself.
- Channel what a good friend would say to you about your thoughts and listen to that perspective. Reframe the hypothesis or story to a more accurate one.

4

Balancing yourself in the equation

It's a truth universally acknowledged that there is a mind-blowing amount of 'stuff' to hold in your head when you are a working parent. I love the description that it's like having 25 apps open simultaneously in your head. It feels accurate as the multiple demands, activities and responsibilities compete for your attention. It is easy to feel overwhelmed when they are all running at once with notifications pinging left, right and centre and decisions and action being required on everything. There is more to cope with in terms of tasks, information, emotions, logistics, communications, demands and activities. We're going to look at mitigating the mental load, the perils of perfectionism and grappling with guilt shortly.

However, there is another narrative here too, about 'more than before' in the AC world, which can be overlooked. It is not just that there is more than before to do or to cope with. You *are* more than you were before. Parenting is a strength.

You are more than before

What you bring to work is greater than before precisely because you are a parent. There can be a sense of being or feeling less at work because we hold split responsibilities across the different aspects of our lives: perhaps less time at work, maybe working a part-time pattern. And the same at home: we can feel like there is a deficit because we are spending time and energy at work. I would argue that both elements of the equation are multipliers. We bring confidence, fulfilment, skills, perspective and more to home as a result of our experiences at work. And we bring similar things and more to work because of our role as parents at home.

Another frequent question new parents return to work with is:

'What if I'm not as good as I was before?'

It is human, relatable and understandable for self-doubt to creep in about how you're going to manage this new era, and for you to wonder if you will be as effective and successful as you were before your world expanded. It is normal to wonder if it will be possible to catch up on all the changes in people, technology, clients, teams, acronyms and ways of working whilst you've been out on parental leave. And it is understandable to question if that fabulous reputation you had before children will disappear now you have new priorities.

I cannot say loudly enough or with enough feeling that you are *more* than you were before.

There can be a sense for parents that there is some kind of deficit to be made up for, not just at the start but throughout the parenting journey. The reality is that at the return from parental leave and far beyond, working parents bring so much more to their jobs as a result of being parents.

What might the marketing be for the development programme that is currently called parental leave? It's far from a long holiday, as we know. Whilst it can be an amazing period of bonding and extended time with your little one(s), it is an incredibly stretching period of growth. Not every day is filled with high-quality time and special moments. Some days it is just about getting through to bedtime, and the skills needed to navigate the day (or week or month) are varied. Imagine the advertisement:

'Looking for a high-impact, fully immersive, transformational development programme that builds resilience, emotional intelligence, innovation, risk management, efficiency and communication skills? Try the Parental Leave Programme!'

Parental leave is surely one of the most stretching periods of development. Keeping a small human alive and learning how to parent when there is no manual and the stakes are so high is a huge learning curve. Resilience is tested and new strategies to cope are developed. Dealing with ambiguity, innovation, stakeholder management, risk management and communication shapes daily life. If we are parenting other small humans as well as a new baby, that's a whole other growth story too. All these new skills, capabilities, mental strategies and deeper empathy positively impact our ability to be brilliant at work.

Seasoned working parents are some of the most efficient and effective employees you will meet in the workplace, precisely because they've learnt to prioritize ruthlessly. They know how to focus in intense bursts, not sweat the small stuff, rise above toddler-like outbursts and actually delegate properly because they simply can't do it all themselves. As Anna, a director in professional services, notes:

> *'I became better at work after having children because I was more focused, more ruthless with my time, more assertive and demanding of what I wanted because I felt like if I'm leaving my children, I want it to be for something good.'*

As parents navigate all the ongoing milestones as their children grow up, there is constant new learning, deployment of different skills and an evolving perspective. As another working parent, Carolyn, puts it:

> *'Having teenagers means I am now an expert in negotiation. And I know how to dig deep when I am already tired in order to listen properly and be there, because if I don't, I might miss "the thing" they really need me for.'*

Why is it that teens choose the point at which bedtime is tantalizingly close and you are practically on your knees to open up about that really important thing that's on their mind? We grab the moment or else they might not talk to us about it at all. Being able to focus and be present, having the ability to switch from the easy-to-reach *tell* mode to step back into *ask and listen* mode is a vital skill in helping your children to talk and think well and it's equally valuable at work.

We are more equipped than before as parents. Research conducted by Rutgers Business School found caregiving experiences improved workplace skills significantly across 18 categories, with the top 4 being empathy (49%

improvement), efficiency (38.9%), persistence (33.6%) and prioritization (29.8%).[13]

A quick look at some of the leading business schools in the world demonstrates the kind of leadership capabilities that are in sharp focus for developing future leaders. The International Management Development Institute highlights eight key leadership skills that are vital for business success.[14] It's not hard to translate the skills we grow at home with our children, at every stage, to these skills we need at work.

Eight leadership skills we also build at home

Scan the below, perhaps with a wry smile, as you reflect on how you deploy these skills at home (for 'client' or 'employee', read 'baby, toddler, child or teenager'):

- **Relationship building**: forging strong working relationships with employees and clients through honest communication and genuine care, and by understanding aspirations and strengths.
- **Agility and adaptability**: being able to adapt to both internal and external changes – even if that means working outside of your comfort zone.
- **Innovation and creativity**: innovation begins with ideation – the phase where outstanding ideas are

[13] Lisa S. Kaplowitz and Kate Mangino, 2023, https://hbr.org/2023/08/research-caregiver-employees-bring-unique-value-to-companies

[14] *The 8 Key Leadership Skills You Need to Know in 2025*, 2025, https://www.imd.org/blog/leadership/leadership-skills/

developed and become the foundation of innovation success.

- **Employee motivation**: being able to continuously motivate employees, which requires leaders to be connected to their teams and attentive to what is going on around them.
- **Decision-making**: strong decision-making skills, having the conviction to stand by your decisions, whilst also recognizing the need to adapt when those decisions do not lead to the desired outcome.
- **Conflict management**: being good at identifying conflict and have foresight on how to resolve it. Managing to stay rational when faced with confrontation.
- **Negotiation**: knowing how to find the best long-term solution by getting the most out of two different sides in order to achieve organizational goals.
- **Critical thinking**: making a lot of difficult decisions, often under pressure: the ability to think clearly, whilst building a logical connection between different ideas.

A quick strengths audit can reveal things we have just chalked up to experience and overlooked.

Activity #10: More than before

Against this initial list of work-relevant capabilities, write down the ways in which being a working parent adds to your level of experience and skill.

If you think of something you are stronger in as a result of parenting that is not included on the list but important to your work role, add that in.

- Empathy:
- Prioritization:
- Communication:
- Project management:
- Delegation:
- Resilience:
- Relationship management:

Reflect on your observations and consider what this means regarding your value to your workplace

And vice versa. How might your strengths at work serve you at home with your growing family?

Human professional or professional human?

Working in a long-term sustainable way means we need to reconcile both the professional and the human in us. Putting AI to one side, everyone at work is human and most of us want to be authentic at work. Both the human and professional elements of our personal equation need our attention if we are to last the distance and enjoy the race.

When we sacrifice our human needs and experiences at the altar of professional perfection, it leads to burnout. When we over-index on human at the expense of professional credibility, it can lead to career limitation.

Maybe, for some of us, being a parent helps to introduce better balance rather than prevent it. A Dad who works a 4-day week, has a neurodivergent primary-aged child, a toddler and holds a significant part of the childcare and domestic load said this:

> *'To be honest, ironically, I would probably have had a massive burnout issue if we had decided not to have children. I would have carried on running full-pelt forever and blindsided myself into a brick wall. Having kids rewired my brain; kids have taught me the futility of trying to control everything. You can't get a small person who doesn't want to go to the toilet to go to the toilet. Having enough humility to exist in the world without believing I can control everything has helped. I am less of a perfectionist and without kids I would have gone on a lot longer without having any kind of self-awareness about that.'*

Perhaps the fact we are working parents can be a positive factor in better understanding what we need to let go of and maybe even catching ourselves before burnout.

Most of the working parents I meet are sure of their commitment to the 'professional' part of the equation. Sometimes, they are hiding the part of themselves that is more human, maybe vulnerable, especially if it's connected to what is happening at home with the family. We can be unsure of what is acceptable in terms of sharing the human side of the equation at work. Is it effective and professional to show some of what's going on in the home space? We know that few people want all the details of how wild your sleep-deprived night was, how narky your teenager is or how dire that diabolical nappy was you dealt with first thing. And yet, maybe there is scope to share more of our lives as parents?

There is a movement towards openness and honesty. We are hearing more real stories, which is important if we are to shift to a human approach to leadership and to our experience of work. But there is the pitfall of over-sharing too: the over-emphasized storytelling on the human side of people's equations. The kind of sharing that tips away from admirably honest and useful to awkward, irritating or draining. The human story to the exclusion of the professional wears thin fairly quickly.

Many of us instinctively know the balance when it comes to not over-sharing, but we tend to lean to professional over human and perhaps overdo that, because we are worried what people will think of us. When we are rarely open about what makes us who we are, the ways in which we are challenged and the things we get wrong, there is a risk that we seem to be perfect, unassailable, invincible even. This can get in the way of trust and connection.

As we consider 'The Working Parent Equation', here is another useful equation. 'The Trust Equation'[15] is a simple, yet effective way to look at how we build trust in relationships. It was developed for the Trusted Advisor in business and has resonance for all of us:

$$Trust = \frac{Credibility\ (C) + Reliability\ (R) + Intimacy\ (I)}{Self\text{-}Interest\ (SI)}$$

[15] David H. Maister, Charles H. Green and Robert M. Galford, *The Trusted Advisor*, 2001.

Essentially, for there to be deep trust we need to feel that all the things on the top line are present and for there to be an absence of what's on the bottom line.

If you take a moment to reflect on a time you have built a deep, trusted relationship at work, can you see how these elements were in place?

- You found the other person was **credible** (their track record, knowledge, expertise, experience, qualifications, etc.).
- You saw they were **reliable** (they did what they said they would do, when they said they would do it).
- You felt you knew them (they shared something about their life, maybe a vulnerability; you felt you saw the authentic them) – this is **intimacy.**
- You sensed they were not on their own agenda but were genuinely interested in you and what you needed to achieve – they were not oozing **self-interest.**

And when we think of the relationships where trust is lower, there will be one or more of these elements of the equation missing from the top line and/or self-interest will be present. When we get more than a whiff of self-interest in the other person it immediately diminishes trust (think bad sales!).

Intimacy is an odd word to consider in the work context but what we mean here are those points of authentic connection where you feel you get a real sense of that person. It's not a tell-all, indiscriminate approach but a willingness to show up as who we are and share moments of vulnerability from time to time that makes us human.

What we choose to share in the intimacy part of the equation can be the difference between inappropriate over-sharing on one end of the spectrum and buttoned-up invulnerability at the other end. There is a balance to be had. When we pair intimacy with low self-interest, it helps to keep us in the most effective zone. We are aiming to be the kind of professional who can connect brilliantly and doesn't burn out or sink under the weight of maintaining a pretence that the kids only exist between the hours of 6pm and 6am and at weekends.

As her child began school for the first time, Jemma felt an overwhelming sense of relief and gratitude when another working parent shared how hard it was for her child at the same point. Amidst all the shiny front-door first-day-of-school photos on social media, it can be a fraught and emotionally charged time. It's even more powerful when managers are able to empathize and offer flexibility to team members facing into the big parenting milestones. Whether it is starting school for the first time, beginning high school or public exam season for teenagers, these chapters are defined by exhausted children, new routines and an emotional rollercoaster for children and parents alike.

There are different shades of human professional challenges that Dads work through, specifically. The expectation is often still that mothers carry the majority of childcare responsibility, so when Bernardo Lu-Tsu needed to be at home for his sick child, there was surprise and 'can't your wife take care of him?'

Anna was asked at an international conference by another woman: 'Who's helping your husband with the kids while you are away?' And when Anna responded he was doing it alone, the reply was: 'Oh well, at least he will suddenly see all the things you do when you are there!' Anna explained that he was already doing it all of the time. There is still much to do to normalize the involvement of Dads with their children.

Genuine and judicious openness can be a game-changer for you and others at work. It can help you to reset with clarity on what being a human professional looks like for you as a working parent, a colleague and a manager. It could make all the difference to the next generation of parents coming up behind you.

Activity #11: Your version of human professional

I invite you to write down your responses to the following questions. It may help to think of other working parents you've observed whose example you have appreciated. There may also be examples you've observed where the balance was not effective.

Answer the questions with the Trust Equation in mind, especially around *intimacy* which is often the element we feel most conflicted about, but which has the power to turbocharge relationships at work. Maybe there are certain milestones in your own parenting journey which you wish someone at work had been more open about?

- I will share more with others at work about…
- I choose not to share with others at work about…

- As a working parent, I want to role-model…
- As a working parent, I don't want to role-model…
- One new thing I will do to increase my honesty at work about working parenthood is…

Everyone's responses will look different. The key is to be authentic to your way of going about this and to challenge yourself on where you would benefit from dialling up or down the human and professional elements to increase your effectiveness.

Getting a grip on guilt

Guilt seeps pervasively into so many elements of our lives. Working parents express guilt about the time they are not giving to work, the time they are not giving to their families, the ways they are not enough, the ways they let others down, the ways they are not looking after themselves, the ways they are neglecting their partners… and the list goes on.

Guilt may have a role to play in nudging us to see opportunities for positive change by pricking our conscience. Maybe something is out of balance that requires our attention and there is a useful nugget for us to pay attention to. However, more often than not, guilt is less a helpful nudge and more an untamed, misdirected force which holds us back and drains our overstretched resources. After all, if we've done the audit on why we are balancing work and family and what our AC (After Children) success criteria look like, we need to understand what it is we feel most guilty about and how much of this is grounded in our own definition of success versus what we think others expect of us.

In my experience, working Mums bring guilt into coaching on a more regular basis than working Dads. Is it that men do not feel such an acute sense of guilt or is it that they are just not ready to talk about it? More research is needed to better understand this. What I have heard in my research for this book is that there is no universal principle; guilt seems to manifest for all parents in differing ways.

The baby boy Laura had spent every day with for a year was now at nursery full time. Laura was asking herself if it was the right thing. How would she know he was really OK, given he couldn't speak yet? He couldn't tell her how he felt or what it was like for him. She also felt guilty that she wanted to continue operating at the same career level at work.

How did Bernardo Lu-Tsu feel about guilt after taking shared parental leave and returning to work? He references the 'heart-breaking' feeling of his son being in nursery for long hours every day and wishing he could spend less time there. However, being pragmatic meant less guilt about what he terms the 'economics of the situation': the necessity for both he and his wife to work full time and send financial support to family. Plus, there was no local family ecosystem of childcare support that they could tap into.

Sofia, a new mum who recently adopted a daughter with her husband, reported feeling 'zero guilt' about the big picture of being at work. She is driven predominantly by a desire to role-model to her daughter the importance of female financial independence and she does not feel guilty about being at work full time. But she does feel:

'1,000 small guilts every day.'

She feels guilt about what she has not managed to do for her daughter, whether it's delaying making a non-urgent doctor's appointment or not having what she considers the right outfit washed and ready in time for a special nursery event. The everyday sense of guilt that she might be dropping a ball is real.

Carl, a senior level consultant, recalls feeling he was not doing a good job at work or at home as he juggled a client-facing role with being a Dad to two children. Guilt was not a word he used, but he described the tensions of feeling he was letting people down in both of these areas of his life with the result being a high degree of stress.

When her eldest started school, Layla was on an extended leave of absence, which her company offers to all employees after a number of years of service. Starting school heralded a period of bad dreams and bed-wetting for her daughter as she adjusted to the change. Layla notes she would naturally have defaulted to guilt that her career was the cause of her daughter's reaction had she not been away from work:

'I know I would have blamed myself if I had been at work at this point and not on a Leave of Absence, so that's been interesting to see and reflect on.'

Dom, a head of department in a bank, who shares the parenting duties equally with his working wife, describes it as 'letting his team-mate down' if he needs to change their finely balanced schedule. When a last-minute presentation needs to be finalized for the Executive Team or there is a sudden need to be in a different part of the country, he feels guilt about not sticking to the plan, not being there for dinner with the kids and not being there to relieve his wife, who on that day may be balancing working from home in her own senior role, picking up children from school and then running the evening gauntlet.

Guilt about not being enough at work or at home is common. Anita, a single parent, remembers intense feelings of guilt hearing her daughter say, 'Why are you at work so much, Mummy?'. There was no other option; Anita was responsible for the financial security of her family. She ran an extended marathon every day of settling her child, who found it especially difficult with autism to be left at nursery or with childminders, and then racing to work to be there on time, long before COVID-19 had shifted the world of flexible working for the better. When I asked her how she dealt with the guilt, she honestly replied:

> *'I don't think I did. I just had to get on with it. We needed me to be working full time. I put my energy into making sure the time we did have was brilliant, doing as much as we could together.'*

And she also reflected that work brought essential confidence, which gave her greater resilience to be the Mum she wanted to be when being a single parent was really tough. Feeling guilty about it was to overlook the benefits her career resourced her with financially and emotionally, all of which was part of providing for her daughter.

Clare, a solo parent with a senior job in retail, also describes the intensity of this feeling when you are 'it' for your child. Knowing you are the sole parent added to her sense of pressure to be there all the time and cover all the bases brilliantly. She felt guilty if she was ever not there at bedtime for her school-aged son, because she was not in a position to be sharing bedtimes with a partner. It took a while to give herself permission to arrange childcare for part of the week to enable her to be home later than bedtime or to cover some mealtimes before she could get home from work. She simply could not be there all the time that her son was not at school, and as she articulates:

> *'If I had a partner, they would be doing some of this with my son each week. The fact that it is just me does not mean I cannot share this in any way with anyone else ever.'*

Psychologists and researchers are helping us understand the crucial role of getting more specific about what we feel in order to find clarity more quickly. Responding with self-compassion rather than self-criticism enables us to get a more accurate version of what has happened and come to a more reliable conclusion. Guilt might have something useful to tell us or, as the author Brené Brown puts it, it may be shame in disguise 'because where shame exists, empathy is almost always absent':

> *'We feel guilty when we hold up something we've done or failed to do against our values and find they don't match up. It's a psychologically uncomfortable feeling, but one that's helpful. The discomfort of cognitive dissonance is what drives meaningful change. Shame, however, corrodes the very part of us that believes we can change and do better.'*[16]

[16] Brené Brown, *Dare to Lead: Brave Work. Tough Conversations. Whole Hearts*, 2018, p. 129.

We need to bring in our inner scientist, historian or journalist and add kindness to the mix. We can turn guilt into something much more positive: clarity, compassion and action. We can see guilt as a guide, not a verdict.

Activity #12: The Guilt Compass

Reflect on a time when guilt got a grip on you. What happened that brought up the feeling of guilt?

Step 1: Identify the moment of guilt

For example, missing bedtime, not being at a work event, your kids missing an extracurricular activity they love doing.

Step 2: Is this guilt helpful or harmful?

Does it help you spot a mistake that you can repair, or is it shame in disguise?

Helpful guilt	**Harmful guilt**
'I acted outside my values and I can repair it'	'I feel like a terrible person'
It points to something fixable or a boundary to pay attention to	It leads me to feel I am not enough
It motivates me to reconnect or take action	It makes me withdraw, shut down or self-blame in a harsh way

Step 3: Self-compassion reframe

Talk to yourself as you would to a good friend. For example:

- 'I'm feeling guilt. Guilt is hard.'
- 'All parents feel this way sometimes. I am not alone.'
- 'I am doing my best. I can make a small change next time.'

Step 4: Align with your values

- What key value of mine is visible underneath this guilt?

For example, patience, presence, responsibility.

- What's one small action I can take today to respect that value?

For example, apologize to someone, play together for 10 minutes, detach from someone else's decision.

When we pause and understand the message behind the guilt, we can respond more positively.[17]

The myth of perfection

Perfection lies somewhere out there for us if we can just learn enough, do enough, know enough, change enough, try

[17] For a more in-depth exploration of shame and harmful guilt, see Brené Brown, *I Thought It Was Just Me (but it isn't): Making the Journey from 'What Will People Think?' to 'I Am Enough'*, 2007.

enough and be enough. We are tempted to strive to be the perfect parent, the perfect worker, the perfect partner.

> *'You think before you have children you will be one of these amazing parents where the kids are always sharply dressed, hair brushed and they're going to school playing the flute whilst walking. You quite rapidly change that expectation. It's more like, everyone's still alive, no-one is completely covered in their own excrement and you're trying to retain some of your own sanity in the mix.'*
>
> (Tom, director in the energy sector)

Perfection appears to be tantalizingly close as we absorb all the different ways others tell us to achieve it. Whilst perfectionism is primarily an internal thinking pattern, the influence of seeing what we believe to be others nailing life makes us feel lesser and inadequate. We are tempted to buy into the idea that perfection is achievable as we get fed with videos, podcasts, posts, reels, books, articles and celebrities showing us we can look better, eat better, feel better and be better people.

However, we have the opportunity to select what we absorb and to see 'perfect' for what it is: a myth. The key is to find out and believe that our best is good enough. In fact, that our average is often good enough. We are enough. Sure, we can always improve or learn something new but that is distinctly different from setting an unattainable bar of perfection that we buy into without really questioning it because others seem to tell us it's possible. Aiming high is different from demanding perfection.

All of this can exacerbate a fairly common way of thinking: perfectionism. Being a working parent notches it up a gear. We just can't seem to step back enough to be convinced that 'done is better than perfect' or to embrace the 80/20 rule (the Pareto Principle[18]), the idea that 80% of the outcomes derive from 20% of the tasks and be prepared to let the rest go. As Kristin Neff puts it,

> *'Perfectionism is defined as the compulsive need to achieve and accomplish one's goals with no allowance for falling short of one's ideals. Perfectionists experience enormous stress and anxiety about getting things exactly right and feel devastated when they don't.'*[19]

Perfectionism is not a mental disorder although maladaptive perfectionism can lead to high stress, relationship difficulties and burnout. If you notice that perfectionism is interfering with daily functioning (for example, intrusive thoughts or a constant feeling of being a failure), it is best to talk to a medical professional for advice. For the majority of people, perfectionism not dangerous but is a trait that can benefit from being tamed.

It can manifest as setting excessively high standards for ourselves, critical self-evaluation, expecting too much of others and over-reliance on external validation. Brené Brown writes that when we grow up being praised for achievement and performance, we adopt a 'debilitating belief system: *I am what I accomplish and how well I accomplish it*'. That's food for thought for all of us as parents as we consider how we praise and what we praise our children for. Brown continues:

> *'Perfectionism is not self-improvement. Perfectionism is, at its core, about trying to earn approval… Perfectionism*

[18] See Pareto's 80-20 Rule Theory, n.d., www.businessballs.com/planning-workload-time-management-and-prioritisation/pareto-80-20-rule-theory/

[19] Kristin Neff, *Self-Compassion: Stop Beating Yourself Up and Leave Insecurity Behind*, 2011.

is not the self-protection we think it is. It is a twenty-ton shield that we lug around, thinking it will protect us, when in fact it's the thing that's really preventing us from being seen.'[20]

If perfectionism is a 'twenty-ton shield that prevents you from being seen', how helpful is it? We can find ways to let go, be real and be seen. Lessening the hold perfectionism has over us requires us to:

- Loosen comparative assessments
- Increase self-compassion
- Exist more in the moment
- Increase our gratitude

We'll look at these things in turn.

Comparison is the thief of joy[21]

When we spend energy comparing ourselves to others, it rarely ends well. Social media exposes us to comparison on

[20] Brené Brown, *Dare to Lead*, p. 79.

[21] 'Comparison is the thief of joy' is a phrase attributed to Theodore Roosevelt.

steroids, without the balanced perspective of how things are in reality. We'll look at how you may need to lessen your exposure to social media in Chapter 8. Then there are the people around us: other parents, colleagues, leaders, friends. It is natural to look at others and compare how we stack up. Sometimes we see different ways to do things and learn a new idea; social comparison theory acknowledges that friendly competition and comparison can lead to motivation and self-development.[22] However, more often than not, we focus on the ways we are lesser and assume that others have something better.

We can reduce the negative impact of comparison with others by acknowledging that we may be comparing ourselves unrealistically to someone who has a real strength in an area that we do not. Maybe we are comparing the social life of someone who is very sociable with our own, when we are naturally much less sociable than they are. We can also acknowledge that we do not know the whole story as others often mask the reality. Might that parent who seems to have part-time work sorted actually be pedalling like mad beneath the surface to keep afloat and feeling vulnerable?

Being curious and asking how others are finding things can open up reassuring and helpful conversations about the collective struggle that so many working parents experience, along with shared learning and useful ideas on what has worked well.

[22] Social comparison theory is the idea that individuals determine their own social and personal worth based on how they stack up against others. The theory was developed in 1954 by psychologist Leon Festinger.

Self-compassion

The way we talk to ourselves is important. If compassion is something you struggle to conjure for yourself, I recommend exploring it further. Kristin Neff's work is a good place to start.[23] The science behind how we behave now and how we were parented, attachment theory and the ways we can increase our kindness to ourselves is fascinating. In short, Neff points out:

> *'Choosing to relate to ourselves with kindness rather than contempt is highly pragmatic.'*[24]

The research literature finds that people who are more self-compassionate tend to be less anxious and depressed. We are primed to focus on negative information so that we are alert to threats in the natural world; it's part of keeping safe. However, negative thoughts tend to echo in our minds, leading to rumination which shuts down our ability to think well and be resourceful. Learning how to be kinder in our thinking is crucial. We will look at this in more depth as we turn to the inner critic in Chapter 10.

Being present

For all of us, noticing what is happening in the moment and being present is key to dialling down perfectionism. If mindfulness practice doesn't come easily to you, why not start small and work up.

For example, a 5-minute break outside in the fresh air focusing on birdsong or the colours you can see around you

[23] Kristin Neff, *Self-Compassion.*

[24] Neff, *Self-Compassion*, p. 51.

can quickly bring us into the present. Two minutes of slower breathing and paying attention to your breath, putting your feet flat on the floor, grounds us. Finding ways in the course of your day to tune into awareness of what's happening in the moment reduces stress and calms the system down; ultimately it makes us more joyful and more effective.

If you're at home and the kids want you to play with them but you're feeling drawn back to work, agree with yourself that you will give 15 minutes of high-quality attention and presence over 30 minutes of half-hearted, distracted time where you have one eye on the phone and work issues and one eye on the game. You may even find you extend the time because your inner perfectionist has quietened down enough to let you. Being present is a terrific antidote to perfectionism.

Gratitude

When we are caught in the grip of perfectionism and believe that we must plough on and do more and that we are not doing or being enough, it is very powerful to refocus from deficit to abundance.

Saying or writing down what you are grateful for is a fantastic reset.

Sara found this worked well on the train commute. Instead of doing emails, she took 5 minutes to look out of the window and name just 3 things she was thankful for that day. From as small as, 'I can feel the warmth of the sun on my face' to 'I am grateful for my healthy family'. Another way to apply this is by writing down the things you are grateful for just before you go to bed. Flipping the internal narrative from all the things you have not got or feel you are falling short on to all the things you are grateful for is like flicking a switch. If you find sleep elusive, this could be a key part of how you prepare for bed.

Activity #13: Thankful for 3 things

Pause and take a few breaths. Notice something nearby and focus on it. Perhaps it's a view, a colour or a sound.

Reflect on 3 things you are truly grateful for in this moment. Write them down. If you feel compelled to write more, add to the list.

1.
2.
3.

What does this tell you about what is good right now?

If you are able to dial down perfectionism, there will be a positive knock-on to your ability to rest. If you can shift from a sense of 'lack' to appreciate what you already have, you will ease feelings of inadequacy. If we let go of some of the things we are putting undue pressure on ourselves to achieve and be, we will see the opportunities for dropping a couple of things, delegating a few more things and sharing the load more.

Nuggets from Chapter 4

- You are more than before, not less. Reflect on what you are bringing to work because you are a parent. What are you bringing to home because of your career?
- How much of a human professional are you? Review the Trust Equation to help you consider ways to build trust at work and avoid over-indexing on unhelpful things.
- Get a grip on guilt: assess if it is helpful or harmful guilt by using the Guilt Compass and choosing a response.
- Be present more: try out a mindfulness practice or start small by:
    - Noticing something outside your window
    - Tuning into a sound you can hear
    - Noticing your breathing and how your body feels
- Make it a daily habit to spend a few minutes writing down what you are thankful for, however small. What does this tell you about what you have versus what you lack?
- Talk to yourself as you would to someone you care about: dial up self-compassion in your self-talk.

Part 3

Prioritization for professionals

'Once you stop believing that it must somehow be possible to avoid hard choices about time, it gets easier to make better ones.

You begin to grasp that when there is so much to do, and there always will be, the only route to psychological freedom is to let go of the limit-denying fantasy of getting it all done and instead to focus on doing a few things that count.'

(Oliver Burkeman)

5

Balancing priorities across your equation

Am I urgent or important?

For a while, I had a sticky note planted on my home computer of the Eisenhower matrix. It's an oldie but a goodie; you may be familiar with it. It's a 2x2 matrix reputedly developed by General and President Eisenhower for prioritizing tasks into what is urgent/not urgent and important/not important.

My then 9-year-old had been in my home office, doing her homework on Google Classroom, and had spotted this sticky note. She had decided to make use of the matrix – maybe her homework was not as inspiring as her teachers had hoped? She added her thoughts.

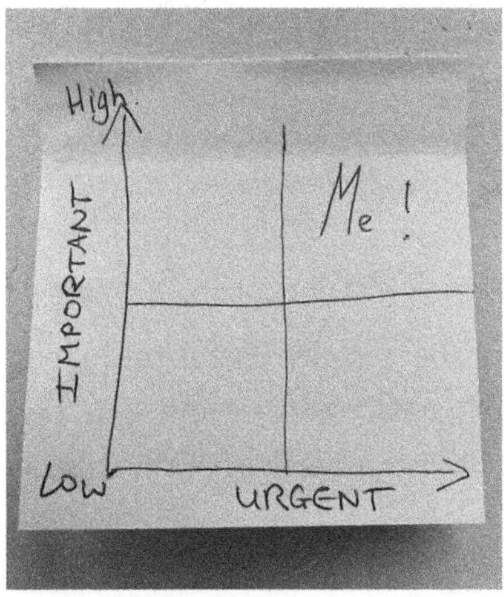

Haha, very droll. And… hmmm.

I felt, in equal parts, proud that she had understood the matrix enough to add her note, amused by her addition and then worried she was telling me I did not prioritize her enough already.

If she meant that she was the 'Me' in the top right box, she was of course right. She and her sister are the most important people in our world… although maybe not always urgent 100% of the time. Knowing her sense of humour, I imagined her saying: 'Hey Mum, I am the most important and urgent thing! *(wink)*'.

But it did prick my conscience. Did she think I needed reminding she was a priority? Note here the Cognitive Triangle at play as I leapt to this thought and my feelings and behaviour followed suit.

Then I felt chastened by the clarity she may have found which outshone my own: what if she had meant 'Me' was me? She and her sister add little notes like 'put your feet up!' or 'have a cup of tea!' to the to-do lists I write for myself containing long lists of tasks and reminders. So, if we follow a similar line of thought, perhaps she had meant I (Mum) needed to be more urgent and important. Then she was, of course, also right.

Was I overthinking it? Undoubtedly. It's the working parent's prerogative.

But it proved to be a really useful prompt in my thinking. Regardless of what she had meant, it is provocative. How many of us would put ourselves in the top right box… ever?

In coaching, this is not something I hear very much and, as we have seen in Part 1, finding ways to carve out space for you is an important part of balancing the equation in a sustainable way.

Eve is a consultant, founder of her own business and solo parent. She says this:

> *'There will be points in time that are about survival. I am a solo parent, not a co-parent, and my life has been so consumed; I have to be the mother and the father. A sense of "me" starts to emerge now my son is a mid-teen. Self-care is the first thing to give. It's not just having a bubble bath. Radical self-care is essential; without it, that is where long-term problems start to take over. I need to step back from societal pressure where other parents' fears take over the way they advise me. My reflection is that I didn't need to hit the wall before I saw this.'*

There's so much to pay attention to in Eve's words, especially on radical self-care and seeing her own needs as urgent and important. Did you also notice her recognition that the fears of other parents create pressure and have an influence on the advice they give? We will come back to choosing who we listen to in Part 4, but it's such a good point that advice is often driven by others' own insecurities. We therefore don't serve ourselves or our children well if we swallow it whole without seeing where it comes from.

How much of what we put in the top right box (the things we categorize as important *and* urgent (i.e. things *we* must *do*) really belong there and what is missing? As much as we love our children, are we prioritizing their every need at the expense of other priorities? What about work: are we prioritizing this above all else? Where are we putting our relationships, friendships, health? Where are we?

Prioritization is challenging and it is easy to fall into the trap of seeing everything in the 'do' box. Working parents are achieving heroic feats every day, often running a marathon before the working day begins. From the moment you wake up (possibly not at an hour conducive to optimum performance if you have small children) through to the time you go to bed, it is full on. Whilst dealing with the complexity and demands of work, parents are expending vast quantities of mental capacity, care and interest in their other big job of parenting.

It is a joy and a privilege to be a parent. It's also a barrage of emotional, physical, logistical and decision-making hurdles that mean you're under constant pressure ranging from mild busyness to heart-stopping levels of stress, sometimes all in the course of a couple of hours. No-one can prepare you for how the emotional connection to your children's mental and physical wellbeing will dominate your own time, emotions, thoughts and behaviour. This is especially true if your children have additional needs or mental health challenges, the strain of which often goes unseen to the outside world. It's literally all-consuming.

Children are beautifully complicated: they wake up in the night, they get ill, they don't stick to schedules, they get sad, they have passions, they have challenges, they have boundless energy. They are learning about the world on a daily basis and sometimes the world is rough and you have to help them pick up the pieces, often when you have literally nothing left to give at the end of a long day.

And given their full social calendars, hands up who can't keep track of the family schedule? It's a smorgasbord of birthday parties, clubs, activities, trips, playdates and sporting, musical and drama commitments, all of which are combined with your own full schedules and commitments.

It takes some pretty good discipline to insert recovery time and rest as top-right-box items. It means having ways to subdue the internal narrative of 'I have to get X done', 'I haven't got time for that', 'it's vital I finish *<insert domestic or child-related or work-related activity of your choice>*'.

Those parents who are both working and performing the primary carer role are under particular pressure. Many parents are doing this alone. Even more respect due. We appear to have disappeared.

Do, delegate, delay, delete

The Eisenhower matrix asks you to be brutally clear and work out which box the things on your list need to go in. It asks you to plot out what must be done soon (by you) and what can be dropped, delegated or scheduled for later.

On one axis is low to high importance (or value). On the other axis is low to high urgency. Everything goes into one of the four boxes on the grid.

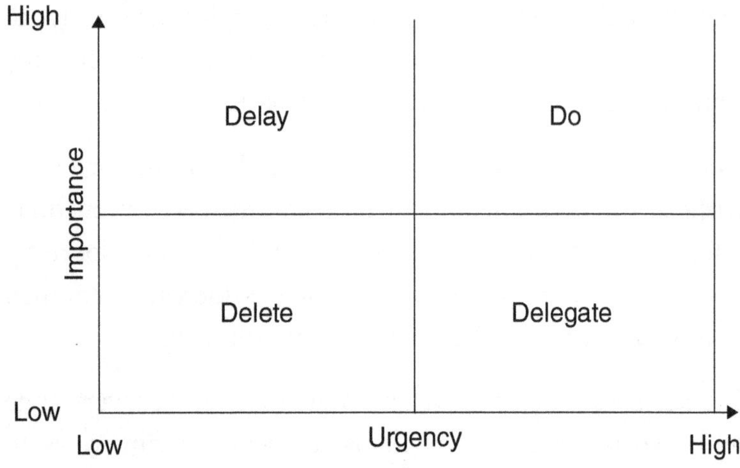

- High importance and high urgency go in the top-right box. These are categorized as things that you need to 'do'.
- High importance and low urgency go in the top-left box. These are things you need to 'delay'.
- Low importance and high-urgency items go in the bottom-right box. These are things you need to 'delegate'.
- Low importance and low-urgency items go in the bottom-left box. These are things you need to 'delete'.

Activity #14: Your Eisenhower matrix

Draw the Eisenhower matrix with some nice big boxes. Plot your current mental list onto the grid. What is in each box? Don't think too hard about it;

just get all the stuff on there and you can come back to where things really ought to be.

Then reflect on your grid with the following questions:

- Which boxes are the fullest?
- Is there a reason why only you are able to do the things in 'do'?
- What could be delegated?
- What feels urgent but on reflection can wait to be scheduled for another time (delayed)?
- What could be deleted? How does it make you feel to delete anything?
- What are you finding hard to place anywhere other than 'do' and why might that be?
- Ask a partner, friend or colleague you trust to take a look at your grid and offer a perspective on any items they think could move.

Blockers to prioritization

You may have a picture of what you need to do, delegate, delay or delete, but no doubt there are sticking points where you have struggled to place items. What gets in the way of us using the matrix as well as we could? Why is it so hard for us to drop things and what makes it difficult to delegate? Whilst the circumstances may be genuinely challenging, there are common pitfalls in the way we think which hold us back. Which of these do you notice getting in the way of your prioritization decisions?

FOMO (fear of missing out)

No explanation needed here. It's the concern that we will miss something or not be part of something. Often we believe it's more important to be there than it really is.

For example:

- 'If I don't take my child to that birthday party myself, I won't be there to meet the other parents and hear what's going on.'
- 'If I'm not in that work meeting, I'll be out of the loop.'
- 'If I mute the school WhatsApp thread or ask my partner to monitor it, I may miss a crucial message.'
- 'If I don't join the wider team at the conference, people will know things I don't.'

FOPO (fear of other people's opinions)

Our craving for social approval goes back to when it was critical for our ancestors to be part of the tribe for safety and protection, and our brains are still wired to look to others for validation of our value.[25]

For example,

- 'If I don't attend that meeting, people will think I am flaky and uncommitted.'

[25] Michael Gervais takes an in-depth look at how we trade in authenticity for approval and what happens when we attribute more value to other people's opinions than to our own in his book, *The First Rule of Mastery: Stop Worrying about What People Think of You*, 2023.

- 'If I don't volunteer for that parents' committee event at school, people will think I am above helping out.'
- 'If I go away for a rare weekend with my friends, my parent-in-law will think I am a bad parent.'

Perfectionism

As we saw in Chapter 4, this is the belief that we and only we can do the task well enough and that when we do something, it must always be the very best we can do.

For example:

- 'If I delegate that piece of work, it won't be done to a high enough standard.'
- 'If I don't wash that football kit before training, I'm letting my child down.'
- 'I must cook a healthy and nutritious meal from scratch tonight.'
- 'I can't leave that slide deck where it is: it needs to be perfect.'

Lack of motivation

Overwhelm, tiredness and a sense of paralysis from all the things we think we should be doing can result in a feeling of inertia. The decision-making part of our brains (the pre-frontal cortex) gets fatigued and literally begins to shut down. We either stop doing the things or we stop being proactive in recategorizing the things, because it will require mental energy we don't feel we have.

For example:

- 'I'm too tired to do those things so I will not do any of them.'
- 'It will be too hard and take too much of my energy to delegate that item so I might as well do it myself.'
- 'I'll delay making myself a doctor's appointment until next week. It's not as important as the other things' (… and repeat for 6 months).

When you raise awareness of these influences at play in your thinking, it increases your ability to make decisions on prioritization. The key is to take a hard look at what it is that you and only you can do. If time was infinite, you would perhaps choose to do everything, but time is limited and therefore we can't kid ourselves that we have that option.

Consider what makes that thing legitimately urgent and important and what makes your unique contribution so vital. Learning what to let go of is more important than learning how to do more.

Catch-yourself questions

Wholesale change is hard but you can experiment with 'catch-yourself' questions. If you ask one 'catch-yourself' question at the point at which you are making a prioritization decision, there will be new thoughts to challenge the first thought and help you see new ways forward.

For example:

'I must take my child to sports practice, but I can't find enough space in the schedule.'

'Catch yourself' question…	… leading to different thoughts
'How essential is it that I run my child to that sports practice, or might a friend be able to help with a lift?'	My child would enjoy getting a lift with a friend. My friend will be pleased to help. My friend will know they can ask me to help in the future.
Or	
'How true is it that skipping one sports practice will be a deal-breaker?'	I am not letting them down if we don't go this once. They would benefit from some rare downtime; everyone needs a break.

'I must be in that client meeting but other urgent priorities need my attention.'

'Catch yourself' question…	…leading to different thoughts
'How critical is it that I am in that client meeting?'	This would be a great opportunity for the person in my team to step up and get some brilliant experience. What is the worst that can happen if I am not there and how likely is that?
Or	

'What would happen if we rescheduled the meeting?'	We might all have a higher-quality conversation with more time to prepare. Nothing falls over if we meet another time.

The sticky systems of Chapter 2 also shed light on what might be getting in the way. If we believe we should be doing what others in our previous systems did (bosses, parents, etc.), we may find it really hard to let go of the feeling that we need to do that same thing.

For Jasmine, a senior manager, it was hard to let go of the house being tidy at all times, despite her young family's natural proliferation of toys, equipment and mild chaos. In the family home she grew up in, and where she had enjoyed a secure and happy childhood, her working parents had placed emphasis on an immaculate space.

For Jasmine to drop domestic perfection for time to relax, it would mean lessening her loyalty to the strongest role model of what good parenting looked like for her.

An important factor emerged. Jasmine had grown up in Singapore where having domestic help is more the norm for professional people: a cleaner, a cook, a nanny, a gardener and so on. Where she lived now in the UK, this was not the norm, so comparing her childhood home to her current home was already unreasonable. She needed to let go of a system that was now less relevant in the present. It was clear that a tidy house soothed her and promoted calmness, so it wasn't about throwing away everything; it was finding a compromise on 'tidy enough', not perfect. Her 'catch-yourself' question to shift things across her Eisenhower matrix was 'how vital is it that the house is perfect right now?'

Activity #15: Catch-yourself questions

Consider a prioritization decision you are currently making, which is proving difficult to resolve. If you can hear yourself thinking you 'must' or 'should' do something, pay particular attention to that.

Press pause for a moment and channel your most ruthless Eisenhower perspective. Catch the assumption(s) you are making by asking yourself a 'catch-yourself' question. It may start with one of the following sentences:

- How important is it that…?
- How true is it that…?
- How urgent is it that…?
- What would happen if…?

What positives could come from making a decision to delegate, delay or delete this item? What is possible if you allow yourself to look at things differently?

As Burkeman suggests,

> *'The real measure of any time management technique is whether or not it helps you neglect the right things.'*[26]

It's about deciding what not to do and feeling at peace with that.

[26] Oliver Burkeman, *Four Thousand Weeks*, p. 72.

Giant Jenga for professionals

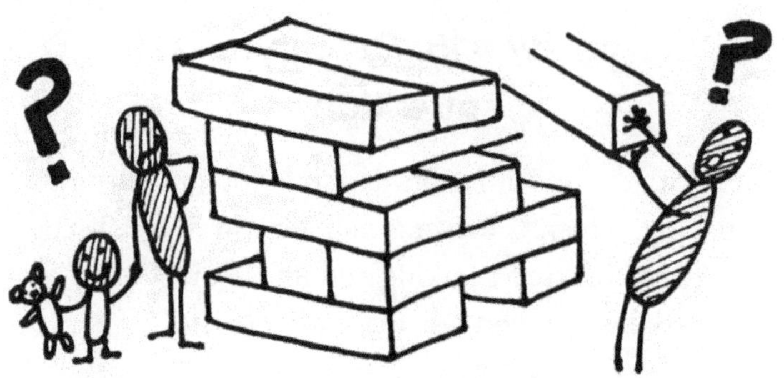

Have you played the simple game of Jenga? There is a tower made of a set number of wooden blocks: three small blocks in each horizontal layer, with each layer laid across the previous layer in a different direction to create stability. The idea is that you take turns to remove one block from the stack and place it on the top of the tower without the whole thing falling down. First one to make the tower fall loses.

Prioritization in working parenthood can feel similar to the giant version of Jenga. We are constantly moving the blocks of time and energy around, often perilously balancing things as we desperately try not to let the whole thing tumble down. The key to success in Jenga is identifying which are the blocks that can safely be removed and replaced elsewhere.

If we imagine for a moment that your time and energy is a Jenga tower, there will be some critical blocks that need to stay where they are and there will be blocks that, with a slight nudge, will slide fairly easily out of the hole they occupy in the tower and can be placed in a new space.

What's helpful about looking at prioritization in this way is the concept that there are only a finite number of blocks in total: your time, energy and capacity are also finite. I know, of course, that you are superhuman and can pull off feats of achievement and dexterity that amaze and astound people who don't juggle all the things you do, but we already know that there is a cost eventually, and that can be the tower losing its stability. It is easy to fall into the trap of kidding yourself that if you take on this, that and the other, you will find the reserves and a way to accommodate it all. 'It's just the juggle', right? Well, yes and no. If it was all doable with no negative impact, you probably wouldn't have picked up this book.

We looked at high-value prioritization in the previous section. To take it a step further, Carol Hugh breaks down parenting into four different types of work in her *Harvard Business Review* article on how strategic the work is and how much it requires direct parental involvement:[27]

1. **Pastoral care**: emotional engagement with your children.
2. **Decision-making**: deciding what is best for your children, problem solving and navigating trade-offs.
3. **Logistics**: transporting children, organizing activities.
4. **Household support**: all the tasks required for running the house, such as cooking, cleaning, laundry etc.

Hugh writes, 'most studies and principles of effective parenting suggest that the latter two need significantly less

[27] Carol Hugh, 2021, www.hbr.org/2021/04/how-working-parents-can-strategically-prioritize-their-time

direct parental involvement'. In other words, they are suitable for delegation where possible.

What would a strategic review of your time and energy reveal to you? If you only have a set number of Jenga blocks (remembering there are only 24 hours in a day and sleep ideally needs to be at least 6–8 of these hours), what shifts will you make to focus on the activities that are highest value to you, your family and work?

If you imagined for a moment that your 'work'-related bricks were blue, your 'family'-related bricks were red and your 'you'-related bricks were green, what would your tower look like? What is the balance of blue, red and green? How do you feel about that?

We may feel 'good parents' are the ones who stay on top of the laundry or escort their kids to every activity. Might good parents outsource what they can afford to outsource or delegate more effectively across family and friends in order to free up time to be present? Might good parents choose strategically which are the highest value activities (e.g. specifically which clubs they will taxi their kids to)? Note that the phrase 'highest value activity' absolutely includes self-care, such as taking a break at times.

Ultimately, we can't and we don't want to let our Jenga tower stand still; life is about continually evolving our particular tower. We need to look for the slack in the stack. Burnout is an extended period of no slack and a very big stack. Anyone who has been close to or entered the burnout zone knows it's hard to stop the stretch and devastating when the tower finally topples over.

So, we need to be strategic. Removing any old brick may not end well. We need to step back and look at which bricks are essential to the stability of the whole. Which are fundamental commitments and where can we remove a brick and create a space without compromising the integrity of the tower? We can continually revisit the stack.

Where are we making space for relationships, our health and strategic career management over getting the day job done? Where can we find time for us? Whether it is time to retreat or time to be sociable, if there is not enough of it in the stack, we are undermining our strength and stability.

Activity #16: Giant Jenga

- If your stack was a Jenga tower, what are the foundational bricks that keep the whole thing stable? Refer back to Activity #2 (80-year-old you) and Activity #4 (work | family | you)
- If your 'work' bricks were blue, your 'family' bricks were red and your 'you' bricks were green, what do you notice about the dominant colours in your current stack?
- What do you want your Jenga tower to look like?
    - What needs to change?
    - Which bricks can be taken out and which can be turned to another colour?

Doorstep diary smash

Parents who share work and family responsibilities describe the constant prioritization and reprioritization as curve balls bounce into the schedule. It's all well and good getting a handle on the big picture but there are so many days when working parents are hit with the unexpected.

Dom describes the moment when all the plans fall by the wayside, and it is emergency prioritization. He coins a phrase I am borrowing with pride: 'doorstep diary smash'. A child is sick literally on the way out of the house to school and you're all on the doorstep. Who is going to stay at home to look after them? Both parents work.

He and his wife get their phones out, ruthlessly assess their individual work calendars for the day and make a quick decision on who can accommodate this grenade more easily, all whilst comforting a distressed child who feels ill. Cue the SOS call to grandparents to see if they can help out (they can't, and for many families this isn't an option). It's prioritization at speed and under pressure. Someone has to stay and make the best of the day around the chaos of a vomiting child and the other one probably feels a mix of relief to be dodging the sickness bullet and guilt that they are not there to help. Let's be honest, probably more relief than guilt when it's a sickness bug!

There are some things we just have to let go of. In the doorstep diary smash scenario, nothing can be done about the child being ill. The parent who stays home and rearranges their diary can let go of the thought that they have let work down.

Instead, remembering the Cognitive Triangle, might these statements be more true and helpful?

- Children get ill and it cannot be helped.
- If I cannot work today, it is not the end of the world.
- Realistically, I am not a critical point of failure at work today.
- It is important my child feels safe and secure while they are feeling ill.
- It is precious time I would not normally have had; if I have to curl up and watch Disney on a loop, so be it.

The parent who leaves their child with their partner or a family member and continues with their work commitments can let go of the thought that they have let their family down. Instead, might these statements be more true and helpful?

- My child is not seriously ill and will feel better soon.
- They are going to get bugs and viruses on a regular basis as they strengthen their immune system.
- I am creating space for my child to build a relationship with another important person in their life.
- I am supporting the family in a different way that is no less valid.

You will have your own experience of the doorstep diary smash. Curve balls are an inevitable part of working parent life and it helps to remind ourselves to expect the unexpected. A couple of 'catch-yourself' questions and alternative thoughts like the ones above are crucial to navigating these curve balls.

And a word to managers. Your response to this kind of scenario can make all the difference to how quickly and confidently working parents reprioritize and stay motivated and effective. You will be repaid a thousand times over for your understanding.

Mitigating the mental load

No book on 'The Working Parent Equation' would be complete without a look at the mental load.

Firstly, what is the mental load? I guess if you're not sure, you probably aren't carrying the majority of it!

It is the mass of the iceberg below the water line: the thinking and activity that lies beneath the observable thing that gets done. It's the hidden labour of anticipating, organizing and executing on all the things related to work life, domestic life, family life and childcare.

There is no doubt that the mental load is a real thing. For parents, it's the never-ending barrage of things that need to be attended to and decisions to be made, from the minutiae of domestic life to the really big ones. We know from neuroscience that the relentless decision-making involved in balancing work and family has a tangible impact on our brains. The pre-frontal cortex (the part of your brain responsible for logic and decision-making) gets tired and begins to shut down, making you feel as if you're wading through treacle. The stress hormone, cortisol, starts pumping around your system.

We enter slightly hazardous waters here as we navigate the concept of the mental load and how this differs between parents. I asked many parents about this idea and will strive to offer as balanced and nuanced a view as possible.

The overriding dialogue in the public domain is that working Mums carry the majority of the mental load. When I speak to working Mums I hear the same thread; an awareness of and sometimes resentment about having to carry so much more in their heads than a male partner. And a resulting level of overwhelm and stress that impinges on their ability to relax, get everything done, focus on what's most important and feel positive towards their partner. We'll hear from different people to try and tread a useful path through this undeniable element of working parent life.

So what is the 'hidden work'? (As if we need a reminder?!)

> *'Experts say that [it] comes in three overlapping categories. There's cognitive labour – which is thinking about all the practical elements of household responsibilities, including organizing playdates, shopping and planning activities. Then there's emotional labour, which is maintaining the family's emotions, calming things down if the kids are acting up or worrying about how they are managing at school. Third, the mental load is the intersection of the two: preparing, organizing and anticipating everything, emotional and practical, that needs to get done to make life flow.'*[28]

When I have coached and interviewed working Mums, I repeatedly hear the distinction between 'planning' (the mental load) and 'execution' (delivery of tasks).

Gail illustrates one small example of this distinction between the 'task' and the 'mental load':

> *'I can delegate taking our child to a birthday party on Saturday, which is helpful. But the real work lies in all the prior WhatsApp communications about little Johnny's*

[28] Melissa Hogenboom, 2021, www.bbc.co.uk/worklife/article/20210518-the-hidden-load-how-thinking-of-everything-holds-mums-back

party, the diary crunching and logistics of getting my child there around Little Gym and getting to Grandma's house for a family celebration and my other two kids' activities. It is the sourcing of the age-appropriate gift or organizing the class collection if we're clubbing together, making sure dietary requirements are communicated and scrambling a lift for another parent who is struggling to make it all fit.'

Another working Mum, Rhian, who is a lawyer, describes how her husband, a marketing director, picks up a large part of the domestic burden and a significant part of the mental load. For example, she rarely thinks about things such as the end-to-end meal-making cycle (from planning to shopping to cooking to clearing up) or any aspect of the laundry. It's on her husband's mental list. They both work full time and have teenaged children.

A UK journalist in a heterosexual relationship experimented with swapping mental loads for a week with her partner; in essence each person went on a week's secondment to the other's role.[29] They found they did not fully understand one another's version of the mental load which ran along fairly traditional gender roles. They concluded the woman had the greater mental load although it was offset to a large degree by the physical work, playing with the kids and financial planning the man undertook.

'It transpires that neither of us thinks the other has it much easier but nor do we begrudge a swap back… We note, too, that our mental loads are so deep-rooted, a complete handover – if, indeed, that is the goal – would require more

[29] Chloe Hamilton, 2025, www.theguardian.com/lifeandstyle/2025/mar/05/i-feel-like-im-on-holiday-inside-our-week-long-mental-load-marriage-swap

than a week's secondment… More important than dividing the mental load equally, is being responsive to what your partner needs and adapting as necessary.'

Clare, a solo parent, notes she carries it all, but equally she does not have the bubbling tension or resentment that someone else ought to be picking up more of it.

'I'm not feeling livid that my partner has not thought to stack the dishwasher.'

She has learnt to delegate things that previously she might have felt she should be doing herself, but it is not easy. She simply cannot cover everything and can't rely on someone else to step in and hold a few things. She has let go of some of the domestic and childcare planning and execution load by seeing the wisdom in recruiting and investing in help at home. As she acknowledges, she is privileged to be able to do this financially. In effect, she has looked at the cost-benefit analysis of outsourcing what she can in order to do more of the things that count the most for her and her child.

Sukh, a divorced Dad of three, recognizes the mental load and also acknowledges that if we were to ask his ex-wife, she would likely reply that she carries the majority of it. The mental load is potentially more nuanced for separated or divorced parents. Rather than debating whether it is more or less intense, there are different challenges. Sukh shares time with the children although the children live with their mother for the majority of the week. For Sukh, who also cares for elderly parents, he is balancing the practicalities of parenting, working and managing his house with significant mental energy directed at helping his teenaged children to navigate life. For example, he spends time encouraging his children to study for exams. Where he and his wife do not share a view, he feels the load sits with him to coach his kids around schoolwork, time management, prioritization and ambition for the future. He is not physically there with them all the time so he is doing this at a distance and without a united parental view. He is spending mental energy and practical time on making this a priority, along with other parenting issues. It is hard because he is not in a position to always be there or work as a parenting team on some things he considers to be crucial.

Heidi, a manager in healthcare who is in a same-sex relationship, recognizes the mental load is weighted towards her. She and her partner have a daughter, they both work and Heidi picks up the majority of the mental load. It's not clear if this is in part because she is the birth mother but she recognizes that her partner carries less of the domestic and parenting-related activity.

Simon and his wife have agreed a split where his wife, a part-time doctor, leads on the parenting and domestic load and he focuses on his career. It's not unusual as part of their cultural norm in an extended family to have 15 people for dinner any day of the week. Bringing people together and organizing this regularly is core to their shared values. Simon acknowledges his wife bears the majority of the domestic and parenting mental load and he carries the responsibility and associated load of creating financial security for the family; they are aligned on this.

There will be thousands of stories where the mental load has never been discussed or it's been raised in frustration and the conversations are far less balanced. Resentment and exhaustion bubbles dangerously close to the surface for many of us when we feel we carry too much.

More often than not, one parent tends to hold the lion's share whatever the relationship looks like, although obviously this is not exclusively so. Perhaps the best route forward is to be intentionally curious about how we and our partner, if we have one, are feeling about it all.

Communication is our friend. If you feel you are carrying a disproportionate load, it's time to talk. Check in on each other to see how you are doing and spot if and where the load needs rebalancing. Could you begin along the lines of: 'I am really feeling the pinch at the moment. How are you feeling about the things you're trying to balance?' If you are on your own, who could you talk to about the pressures you feel and what alternatives might be possible to outsource some elements?

Rhian and Andy, a married couple with a tween and a teen, are dedicated in their forward planning and communication across a 6-week period. They look ahead to any work travel, big events, upcoming work pinch points, children's activities, church rotas and domestic activities. As far as possible, they are clear on who will do what and approach this as a joint undertaking.

Purple jobs

One idea to explore is 'purple jobs'. The idea is that if traditionally gendered tasks can be labelled 'pink jobs' (e.g. cooking, laundry, school admin) or 'blue jobs' (e.g. taking the bins out, financial planning, DIY), what if we threw them all up in the air and labelled everything 'purple jobs'?

Amy, a journalist, and her husband are both in second relationships and have a blended family. They have learnt from what didn't work well in their previous relationships and find purple jobs to be an effective tool, with the following benefits:

- There are no assumptions on who does what and the entirety of the list is visible to both of them.
- Each person elects to pick something up, sometimes including the thing they really don't want to do, but there is an appreciation from the other one for the act of service.
- They can decide together to play to their individual strengths on core jobs they are best suited to whilst remaining open to trying out new things and learning new skills. As Amy puts it, 'anyone can learn how to put up a set of shelves'.

Activity #17: Purple jobs

- What conversation might you need to start with a significant other in your life about the mental load?
- If just one or two things shifted for the better, what would you be sharing more equally or outsourcing?
- How might 'purple jobs' help you talk about the mental load? Itemize the main areas of responsibility and review who is

picking up what and any opportunities for outsourcing where possible. For example: school or nursery administration, childcare arrangements, social events, cleaning, laundry, DIY, finances, family health appointments, birthday parties, extracurricular clubs....

A note on the pitfall of perfectionism... again

All of this may mean you need to ease up on your commitment to things being done exactly as you think they should be done. Ask yourself whether it really matters if another person takes the reins but doesn't do it your way.

I'm far from immune. When my husband took responsibility for most of the morning nursery runs with our first child, he did everything while I commuted to work. On one of the first days, he dressed our daughter for nursery in a t-shirt and tights and nothing else: his later response was 'aren't those leggings?'.

When I picked her up that evening, I felt mortified that our little girl had gone to nursery essentially in her underwear (me: 'What will people think?'). Note the FOPO here. Happily, I can report she had a wonderful day, the nursery staff did not call social services and she did not experience any pain or lasting trauma because her leggings had feet in them that day. With apologies to all parents who have seen Disney's *Frozen* too many times to count, it seems Elsa has a point: we really do need to 'let it go'.

Nuggets from Chapter 5

- Plot out what's on your priority list and be ruthless with what you allow into the urgent and important 'do' box (things that need to be done by you).
- Be aware of blockers in your thinking that get in the way of you being able to delegate and delete items (e.g. FOMO, FOPO, perfectionism, overwhelm).
- Try out a 'catch-yourself' question if you are struggling with a prioritization decision: what else is possible other than your first thought about the situation?
- Visualize your stack of time and energy as Giant Jenga: what is the balance of red, blue and green bricks in your stack? What one or two changes could you make to the colour of the bricks to balance things differently?
- If you feel squashed by the mental load, what conversation do you need to begin as a first step to communicating how you feel? How might a 'purple jobs' approach help you discuss the balance of responsibility across your family?

6

'Yes' and 'no' in your equation

A frequent-flier topic for time-poor working parents is working out what the 'yes' and 'no' decisions need to be:

'I am terrible at saying "no".'

There are lots of good reasons why we resist turning things down and agree to take on additional tasks, responsibilities and activities. In the BC (Before Children) world, this may already have been an issue for you, although you had more capacity and time to absorb more things and perhaps the knock-on impact in your life was less significant. What was hopefully manageable previously is now a higher risk vulnerability if you find it hard to hold the line and say 'no'. Stepping into the breach is so helpful to others and often it opens up opportunity and growth for you, but it can be insidiously powerful in tipping you too close to the edge.

'You need me to attend that client dinner in Edinburgh? I can swap some things around.'

'You would be really appreciative if I could temporarily steer that project that no-one else has capacity to look at? Sure.'

'You're looking for parents to run a stall at the school summer fair and you're desperately short of volunteers? OK.'

'Yes' and 'no': Two sides of the same coin

When I first heard the analogy of the coin, it was such a helpful way to look at this. Let's consider that 'yes' and 'no' are two sides of the same coin. When we call it 'yes' and agree to something, we are simultaneously saying 'no' to something else on the other side of the coin. And vice versa. It's not 'and… and'; it's 'either… or'. When we say 'yes' to something additional at work, we will be saying 'no' to something else at work, or at home, or for you.

Far from being bad at saying 'no', might you be an expert at saying 'no', albeit to the wrong things?

It's all too easy to kid ourselves that we will just find the time to accommodate this extra thing (see Giant Jenga in Chapter 5), but in reality we will be taking time away from some other area of our lives.

When Dom said 'yes' to a last-minute work trip, he was saying 'no' to dinner at home with the family (a key part of their family rhythm), time with his wife and being there to spread the load. On this occasion, having weighed it up, it was the right call. The meeting was a critical opportunity to engage the top team in something high priority.

Another time, he said 'yes' to working on a non-working day and it meant 'no' to spending focused time and being present for his young children on the day he was not supposed to be working. After a few days like these it became apparent the coin needed to be flipped differently.

As parents of older children know, it can be easy to assume at the start that your kids won't need you around as much when they are bigger. They may not need as much physical support from us when they are more independent but the emotional and pastoral role we play grows exponentially. It's tough being a teenager. They need you differently. My learning with teens is that being there is when you catch the opportunities to help them, whether you are driving them somewhere or eating dinner with them or just being in the kitchen as they grab a snack. If you say 'yes' to too many things that take you away from hanging out with them or being near them, you are saying 'no' to building the relationship with them.

Julian is a business owner and father to four daughters: three birth daughters and one foster daughter. His wife is Stepmum to his birth daughters; they are a blended family. He considers one of his greatest achievements to be the fact his grown-up daughters choose to spend time with him now as adults. For example, they often arrange walking trips with him and choose to meet him for coffee and a run on their birthdays. He looks back on the foundations he built over the preceding years in prioritizing a relationship with them as children and teens:

'My children choosing to spend time with me is my definition of AC success.'

There are going to be times you are not there or can't prioritize time with your children. However, if you know deep down that you can and want to be there, try interrupting the perfectionist that is telling you to finish that task or nudging you to say 'yes' to something else and instead ask yourself: 'what would 80-year-old me say was the right call here?' Every time we switch on the laptop to do evening work, we are saying 'yes' to our work and saying 'no' to strategic recovery time, relationships, domestic necessities, health or other things. As we know from Giant Jenga, there are only a finite number of blocks so what we decide to swap around is worth more thought.

People-pleasing

One of the factors that gets in the way of us saying 'no' is our desire to please other people. It's a well-known saboteur. I often hear,

'I know I am a people-pleaser. I wish I wasn't.'

Like many of the drivers in our lives, this will have served us well at times and been a part of our success to date. It is not all bad. However, remember FOPO? Our worry that others will think badly of us can often drive our decisions to say 'yes' to things we know are not helpful to us. When we place pleasing others above our own needs on a continuous basis it's time to step back and look at this again.

Carla was in a senior role working with a difficult client. The client was known to be tricky and Carla's overriding focus was on ensuring that the client was happy. She had begun to work all the hours she could to get through the demanding list of deliverables. The client was driving the project at an alarming pace. Carla was working evenings and some weekends at a cost to her family and her own wellbeing. Others had noticed she was in the firing line more than anyone else and that the micromanagement by the client was unreasonable and excessive. There were pointed references to her being a mother and whether Carla 'had the time' to do things; the client was not a mother.

Carla felt unable to push back on the work, maintain reasonable boundaries or risk disappointing the client. The people-pleasing was on overdrive. The inner critic was telling her she might lose her job, she would be rated as underperforming, that she didn't have enough experience.

When given time to think in coaching, her more helpful and rational mind was able to dispute these thoughts with the truth, which was that she was on a longer-term trajectory for future promotion, she knew her stuff, she had relevant experience needed by the client, she would not lose her job and that she was highly unlikely to be rated as anything below 'meeting expectations'. And 80-year-old Carla helpfully chimed in with 'this client will be irrelevant in your life beyond December. Don't please her at the expense of the people you love and your health.'

Carla came up with 3 small experiments to try out, which were doable, realistic and lower risk than a potential sit-down meeting to discuss the unreasonable behaviour. (That could be Plan B.)

Experiment 1: Next time the client started firing off a list of demands, Carla would switch from agreeing and worrying about disappointing her to 'I can see you are concerned about progress. Tell me more about what's most important to you and we can prioritize together.'

Experiment 2: She would remove the apology from her lexicon. She'd try writing emails and speaking in meetings without 'sorry' or the word 'just' which was minimizing her impact.

Experiment 3: If the client was visibly stressed and distracted on a call (opening her emails, checking Teams chat, using her mobile), making a useful discussion impossible, Carla would ensure her own time was not wasted. She could be constructively assertive: 'I can see you've got a lot on. When would be a good time for us to discuss this?' It was about respecting Carla's time as much as the client's.

Saying 'no'

You can please others but make sure you are also pleasing yourself. As The Speaking Coach, Jefferson Fisher, a trial lawyer who now helps people communicate more assertively puts it, how we speak to others is a game-changer in being heard.[30] We can learn to communicate with confidence. Assertiveness of communication and control of your breath and speech is at the heart of feeling confident when you hold your line.

Activity #18: Saying 'no'

Reflect on a time you have said 'yes' to taking on something new and later regretted it:

- What drove you to say 'yes'?
- What did it mean you said 'no' to?

[30] Jefferson Fisher, 2025, 13:02, https://podcasts.apple.com/gb/podcast/the-diary-of-a-ceo-with-steven-bartlett/id1291423644?i=1000699457581

- What was the result?
- If you had your time again, what would you do differently?

Practise saying 'no' to that previous request. Our fear response can get in the way of how we say it as we are often in 'flight or fight mode' (more on this in Chapter 10) where we speak fast, breathe in a shallow way and look flustered.

Try these 3 things:

1. Remove apology from the way you say 'no' and keep it short: politely decline without the word 'sorry' or making additions such as 'if you're really stuck then maybe I could'. Clear communication is helpful communication.
2. If you experience pushback, remember your needs and be firm by maintaining a polite and assertive tone.
3. Control your breath in order to control your speech. Breathe in for 2 counts, hold it and breathe out though your nose before you speak. Your speech will be more controlled. The short pause it takes to do this also makes the other person believe you are really thinking about what they have asked. Both help you be received as assertive.[31]

[31] For more on this breath and speech exercise, see Jefferson Fisher, 2025, https://podcasts.apple.com/gb/podcast/the-diary-of-a-ceo-with-steven-bartlett/id1291423644?i=1000699457581

Nuggets from Chapter 6

- Think of 'yes' and 'no' as two sides of the same coin: when you say 'yes' you are also saying 'no'.
- Sometimes saying 'no' is not about buying time to do something big. Might it create space to be less busy or to be there for more moments when your child needs to talk or share an important thing with you?
- Combat people-pleasing impulses by reframing who will matter to you most in the future. Channel 80-year-old you to decide who to pay most attention to.
- Practise assertiveness in communicating with others to demonstrate respect for your time:
  - remove apology from your lexicon
  - talk politely and directly about your boundaries
  - call out inefficient use of your time and suggest alternatives
  - breathe and pause before you speak

7

Non-negotiables: Knowing boundaries in your equation

The boundaries between home and work can be difficult to establish and manage. The phrase 'work-life balance' isn't that helpful, implying some kind of either/or utopian see-saw. As we know, it's a complex equation that needs agile adjustments towards healthy rhythms around work and home and ourselves; they are all integrated. There will be times you prioritize a work thing for good reasons and there will be times you prioritize a home thing for good reasons.

Having clarity on what the hard lines are for us is a powerful way to test the 'yes' or the 'no' response and protect the things we value most highly in our lives. Let's look at non-negotiables.

There are the 'no brainer' big things that you haven't ever stopped to question because they are obvious: a child is rushed to hospital and we ditch work to be there. There are the 'no-brainer' routine things: you need to drop your child to their place of education by a certain time every day and whether or not this will be done is not up for debate.

There are hundreds of other calls to make in between hospital emergencies and routine commitments that we are navigating as working parents. What are the lines we are drawing in permanent marker rather than chalk? We need to establish some guard rails that keep us on track as the vagaries of life threaten to derail us. So much is up for negotiation in balancing the equation: compromise and trade-offs are a feature. But there will be some things that are so important to you, your health, your relationships, your work, your children and your family that they deserve to be prioritized come what may.

Carys, a leader in property, always ensures the evening of her children's actual birthdays, whatever day of the week that falls, is kept free. No matter what important organizational event, dinner or programme is going on, she goes home because it happens once a year:

> *'It's just one of our things. It is important to us as a family. I think you find your own ways of slicing and dicing what's important.'*

How to identify non-negotiables

There will be a range of categories, from practical logistics through to psychological wellbeing. Starting small and with simplicity is the best way forward. When we are too ambitious or make things too complex for ourselves it is hard to stick to the guard rails. Even small steps on the most obvious non-negotiables will help to guide your decisions and actions. Whether it is protecting a non-working day, not travelling more than a set number of times a month, exercise sessions or being at home for bathtime a set number of nights, we need to know what and why these boundaries are important to us.

Activity #19: Identifying non-negotiables

What are your non-negotiables? There don't need to be hundreds. In fact, it's better if there are a few really powerful ones that you can stick to.

- What's sacrosanct in the regular rhythm of the everyday? For example, eating lunch; school runs; story time with your child.
- What needs to be protected on a weekly and monthly basis? For example, attending an exercise class; dinner with friends; date night.
- What's non-negotiable on an annual basis? For example, using all your annual leave; visits to family; yearly medical checks; updating your business website.

Review your list and check in on the following:

Check-in question	So what	Your answer
Are these all definitely non-negotiables?	What is the cost to you and significant others if they get traded away on a regular basis?	

Are there any missing non-negotiables?	What might you be overlooking that is really important to you and significant others?	
How many of your non-negotiables support your own health and wellbeing?	What is one thing you need time and space to do that has a positive effect on your wellbeing?	
What does your friend or partner or parent think you should consider adding?	What do they notice about you for the better when you ringfence this thing?	

Take time to look at your diary and work out where you need to block out time to enable these non-negotiables to be protected. What conversations need to happen?

Helen, a senior leader, had traded away an online exercise class, unable to see how she could make time. When she talked to her husband, it became clear that it was entirely possible if she let go of the conviction that she needed to do every bathtime and bedtime. If her husband led on this for some evenings a week, it would not only enable her to do 30 minutes of exercise in the living room but it would also create space for some Dad-daughter time. When she reframed it as such, the guilt receded.

Emily, a leader at a large global retailer, has a hard and fast rule to have a night every month when she meets her best friend; they both have it inked into the diary in advance. Come what may, emergencies aside, they meet for yoga followed by dinner, affording nourishing time, space and social connection.

There will be pressures that test the strength of your boundaries and convictions. If we are not clear about and committed to our personal non-negotiables, it will be easy to concede when they are pushed and we are tempted to prioritize other things.

Two useful things to remember:

1. Test and learn

What we initially establish for ourselves as a non-negotiable may not be as helpful as it first seems and holding ourselves to it can cause unnecessary stress. Carys reflects on the rule she set for herself that the children would not be left in nursery longer than a set number of hours:

> *'If I didn't get there on time for my own deadline, even though nursery continued beyond that time, I felt a real sense of failure. And actually, whilst this was a good guideline for me, it was not a daily non-negotiable in the end. I realized the children were happy there and didn't notice if I was 30 minutes or one hour later on some days, and it meant I arrived less stressed and more ready to be present for the kids.'*

2. Evolution

The non-negotiables we establish are not written in stone forever. Naturally, what's a non-negotiable at one stage of your life may not be so key at another stage. It is therefore an exercise that bears repeating on a regular basis to check what's newly important, what's less relevant now and what needs to remain a non-negotiable. Marga, a Mum of one and a senior engineer in Formula 1 motorsport, is immersed in iteration for peak performance and she puts it this way:

> *'Iterating into the right solution for your particular equation is part of the process. Never see it as a failure but the road to arriving at the best solutions. Like anything in life, it changes and there is a new equation to navigate.'*

Maintaining boundaries

Establishing and maintaining boundaries can be challenging. Communication and consistency are at the heart of how we do this. If you're clearer about what you will say 'yes' and 'no' to and what remains a hard line for you, it will be easier to communicate to others and maintain those boundaries.

In some ways, how we approach this may not be dissimilar to how we work with our toddlers. If you haven't yet reached the toddler-taming stage, good luck! If you are there right now or you passed through this stage a while ago, you will know that toddlers are constantly testing your boundaries to see if you might budge. If you set a boundary and then retreat on it under pressure, the toddler knows you don't really mean it and it's ok to act as if it doesn't exist. Adults are not that different.

Rhianne, whose husband is in the military and away from home much of the time, had a moment of revelation. She had returned to work determined to prove she was still as good as before, taking on multiple responsibilities, hitting every deadline and managing all her family commitments single-handedly. She was close to burnout. In a meeting with her manager, she heard this:

'The thing I love about you, Rhianne, is that you never say "no".'

It was meant as a compliment but Rhianne saw the problem instantly. She was not consistently protecting reasonable boundaries and it had come to be expected at great cost to her wellbeing. She doesn't suggest she was being taken advantage of but certainly she realized if she wasn't consistent and clear, nobody else was going to do that for her. It's not necessarily done with bad intent but managers and colleagues know if you are someone who will bend under pressure, or entreaty, and won't stick to your boundaries. Only you can change that.

What to do about no-man's (or no-woman's) land

Beyond your core non-negotiables, there is a nebulous area we will call the 'no-man's land' or 'no-woman's land' of working parenthood. We're not too sure who this territory belongs to. Is it time for us? Is it time for our families? Is it time for work? Who gets to have it? It is the gaps in between the hard and fast lines and the regular drumbeat of the routine. Often, we have not been able to think in a considered way about how much of this territory we want to relinquish or reclaim or how to do that.

Not everything needs to be or is a non-negotiable and it can be helpful to identify where there are low-stakes compromises: those things you are prepared to trade on at times because it's pragmatic or it buys you credit and opens up something new for you.

Pete, a public relations leader for whom nutrition is a high priority, talks about deprioritizing a homemade meal for a pragmatic frozen pizza on the most fraught evenings. It's not something he wants to do every day of the week but occasionally it's a sensible low-stakes compromise.

Marga is ok with spending time on her laptop after her son is in bed as she leaves work early to collect him and doesn't engage in work again until after he is asleep. Her husband is away travelling for work much of the time. However, she knows she has to switch off with enough time left to relax; solo parenting so much of the time is a long race, not a sprint.

It's relatively easy to prioritize obvious items that crop up temporarily outside of our core non-negotiables, such as the school play where you child has a starring role; we know the right call is to be there. Or it's fairly straightforward to prioritize a key overnight work team awayday, even if it needs careful planning to enable this time away to be possible. Being able to prioritize these things is an excellent start.

When we are operating in the grey area or no-man's land there are potential mines and craters and we feel vulnerable to friendly or not-so-friendly fire. We're picking our route through this landscape carefully, hoping to make good calls on what to prioritize and what to drop, which path to follow and how to dodge the things that will cause damage, all whilst under a degree of stress.

One option is just to run as fast as we can, hoping for the best. This might mean sustaining a punishing pace, reducing time spent on decisions and committing so hard we are close to burnout. Another option is to lie low, hoping it will become clear what to do and keeping our heads down, ready to respond to whatever happens rather than determining the course.

It's a perfect example of how the balancing act of the working parent equation will be different for every person. Where some parents will decide to prioritize every school assembly they are invited to, others will select a couple to attend. Where some parents will always make time for additional 'urgent' conversations with direct reports even when it makes them late to get home, others will decide to only make time there and then for those situations that are highest risk.

Carys says:

> *'I know I don't always make the right call and we get things wrong a lot but it has helped to have a family saying: "what will matter in 6 months' time?". That helps with our guard rails, deciding what to worry about prioritizing and what to let go.'*

Jo, a senior manager in professional services, says:

> *'It's the mental bit that I find hard to place: being physically there with the kids but thinking I should have done this or that. I definitely put the children first in terms of physical presence but mentally I am at work still and I hate that.'*

To help with this she talks to herself which she says sounds crazy but we know Jo is on the right track with those 'catch yourself' questions. She reminds herself:

> *'Look at them, talk about the bubbles in the bath, put your phone down, appreciate their little faces. I'm here with them for a good reason.'*

What's reasonable? And how clearly are we assessing the relative significance of these competing demands on our time in the grey area?

Imagine there are 3 zones:

- non-negotiables;
- low-stakes compromises (things you are willing to trade);
- a grey zone for 'not quite sure'.

Where would you place some recent decisions you've made?

As an example:

Non-negotiables	**Grey zone**	**Low-stakes compromises**
School pick-up 2 days a week. Team awayday. Watching my child in the school play.	Stayed late at work for a conversation and got home late. Skipped an exercise class.	Weekend ballet class traded for family event. Staying 30 mins longer to finish a piece of work rather than doing the pick-up from nursery early.

The items in the middle column will lean more to the left or the right of this grey zone depending on what they mean to an individual and how close they are to 'non-negotiables' or 'low-stakes compromises'.

Activity #20: No-man's land

Draw the three zones on a piece of paper as above: non-negotiables, low stakes compromises and the grey zone. Consider prioritization decisions you've made in the last 2 weeks.

- List the things you would place in the two end zones: non-negotiables and low-stakes compromises.
- Now look at your area of no-man's land or the grey area in the middle. What things have you prioritized recently that sit in this area? Plot them in the middle column, thinking carefully about which side they are closest to.
- Are they nearer to non-negotiables or low-stakes compromises? Try to avoid putting everything centrally and place them nearer to the side that feels like their real home.
- What led you to prioritize these things in the way you did?
- Now you have a bit more distance, how significant are the things that led you to these decisions?

- Reflect on how you feel now about which zone they are in: what can you learn from this?

Nuggets from Chapter 7

- Identify non-negotiables on an everyday, weekly, monthly and annual basis. What are the core things you cannot afford to trade?
- Use check-in questions to see what's missing, what's not as important as it seemed, whether there is enough to protect your wellbeing and what your partner or friend thinks of your list.
- Remember test-and-learn: make changes if you find in practice that something is not as non-negotiable as you thought it was or if something important has been missed.
- Evolve non-negotiables over time. Diarize for 6 months' time to review them.
- Plot recent decisions across three zones and review the grey area. What can you learn for the future?

Part 4

Choosing who to listen to

'Hell hath no fury like a toddler whose sandwich has been cut into squares when they wanted triangles'

(Anonymous)

8

Noisy voices and how to deal with them

Appreciation: What's that?

If only we could dismiss all the noisy commentary on how well (or not) we are doing our jobs as parents and workers. We know that wrangling toddlers is not dissimilar to appeasing a totalitarian despot at times, where nothing we do is right. Hopefully we don't dwell on it because we know their opinion is the product of a developing brain, tiredness and tantrums. We may know that getting a 'thanks', a moment of appreciation, or something other than 'I knowww' from a teenager is a once-in-a-blue-moon event. Hopefully we remember their brains are *still* developing, hormones are raging and they are designed to be self-absorbed much of the time!

More often than not, despite our best efforts, we get responses and results that are far from ideal and it is easy to feel we are falling short. Some days we long for a small crumb of appreciation amidst the chaos. There is rarely a constructive performance review at home; it's unusual to hear 'good job today', especially when you're in the throes of the early years, and the ratio of appreciative to negative feedback can be negligible. If that's how we feel at work too, we are in a tight spot.

Interestingly, The Gottman Institute has discovered that the 'magic ratio' for stable, happy couple relationships is 5 moments of appreciation to 1 moment of what could be better.[32] Yes, 5:1! I suspect many of us would settle for a 1:1 ratio some days. It's food for thought at work as well, especially for managers. How could we be dialling up our appreciation ratio for those we work with? What might even a 2:1 ratio do for motivation and increased performance?

Noise (and silence) can come at us from all directions.

Turning down the volume

[32] Kyle Benson, 2024, www.gottman.com/blog/the-magic-relationship-ratio-according-science/

Sean, a technology leader, discovered this brilliantly polite and direct note left out by his small children. It encapsulates what we might really feel like saying some days: we want to turn down the volume. And beyond the hubbub of home there are many clamours for our attention. Being selective about where we listen is key.

Multiple noisy voices are shouting about what we should be doing, how we ought to go about it, what's best, what others are achieving and what 'great' looks like in practice. We are bombarded with opinions, advice and examples, some of which is meant with good intent, some of which is designed to make us buy stuff, some of which is helpful and some of which is nonsense.

To name but a few sources of noise:

- Social media posts and influencers
- Print and broadcasting media
- Books
- Internet
- Film, TV and documentaries
- Friends
- Colleagues and managers
- Role models
- Family
- Echoes of our family of origin
- Our own inner critic
- Our own thinking traps

It's a mix of other people's opinions and our own inner voice. We will explore the inner voice shortly. For now, let's think about the influence of other people's opinions and how we respond to them. You don't have to look too far to find someone sharing their thoughts on what you *should* do, and it can become increasingly hard to tune into what *you* think and feel about it all.

Carla was newly back at work after her first child, a vulnerable point where she was looking at how others viewed the equation, and advice had a disproportionately significant effect. When a senior client, who did not have children, and someone more senior inside her own firm with children told her the only way to make it all work was to employ a nanny, it had an impact. She had decided a nanny was not the route for her family but hearing senior people tell her that it was the only path to success made her stumble despite her own convictions.

For another parent with a toddler and a school-aged child, a nanny was a great decision for a growing family. However, it took a while to reconcile themselves to pursuing this, due to family members implying that they were 'delegating parenthood' and other parents questioning if the toddler would suffer by not being in a sociable nursery environment. Even when we have thought hard about what we need to do, it can be difficult to stay the course when the noise around us tells us otherwise.

Eve, a solo parent, highlights the impact of others' opinions and how she has created boundaries to protect herself from being swayed by this. She says,

> *'I now choose to let my teenaged son be independent and take himself to school on trains and buses. There is judgement from other parents on why I am not taking him to school. He chose a good school an hour away but I am boundaried about that; it is his decision and I have no guilt.*

Other parents do have guilt on this. When they ask me, "Oh, you don't take him to school do you?" I feel the pang. It has been one of the hard things to not take on their own insecurities. I choose not to listen.'

Choosing who to listen to and who not to listen to is an intentional and active decision we can make.

Swerving social media stress

Social media: love it or loathe it, it's one of the noisiest places we can choose to listen. We are bombarded with opinion, advice, instruction, stories and humble brags. The positive benefits of social media include connection, business development, communities and information. However, the links to anxiety, depression, feelings of isolation, unrealistic expectations and feelings of inadequacy are well-documented. It's an easy way for us to feel bad about our lives, our efforts, our achievements and our success. Excessive use of social media can create a negative self-perpetuating cycle.[33]

If you've ever doomscrolled and fallen down the rabbit's hole of checking your phone, it is worth paying attention to your habits and the extent to which you allow the focus on others

[33] Lawrence Robinson, 2025, www.helpguide.org/mental-health/wellbeing/social-media-and-mental-health

Excessive social media use can create a negative, self-perpetuating cycle:

1. When you feel lonely, depressed, anxious, or stressed, you use social media more often – as a way to relieve boredom or feel connected to others.
2. Using social media more often, though, increases FOMO and feelings of inadequacy, dissatisfaction and isolation.
3. In turn, these feelings negatively affect your mood and worsen symptoms of depression, anxiety and stress.
4. These worsening symptoms cause you to use social media even more, and so the downward spiral continues.

to dominate your thoughts and feelings. Whilst logically we know that we are receiving carefully curated versions of people's lives designed to filter out the reality and emphasize the positives, we swallow it and compare our own day, life, family or achievements to our detriment. We absorb content telling us the right way to do things, the best way to be and the ways we are currently getting it wrong.

It's something we consider carefully for our tweens and teens, but if we think it's only an issue for our children, we can think again.[34] What access is healthy for you? What will you open yourself up to? How can you put guard rails in place that mean you limit what you absorb, how long you engage for and how you will keep a balanced perspective as everyone tells you about their wins and what you must do to be the best person, parent or worker? We need to get strategic.

Activity #21: Social media audit

Review the cost and benefit of social media for you. I invite you to answer the following questions and reflect on your responses. Look at your activity and how it contributes to you feeling well-equipped, well-resourced and confident versus the opposite:

[34] The impact of social media on our children is rightly a high-profile issue. For a deep-dive examination of social media and adolescent mental health, see *The Anxious Generation*, 2025, by Jonathan Haidt, social psychologist and author.

Sources Which social media platforms do you use? (list one in each box). Add more columns if necessary.			
Frequency How frequently do you engage in each one? Hourly? How many times daily? Weekly? Be specific.			
Purpose What is your purpose in engaging? (e.g. staying in touch, marketing, jobs, connections, learning, pleasure, etc.)			

Usage Review what you actually spend your time on social media consuming. Be honest*.			
Alignment To what extent is your actual usage aligned to your purpose in engaging? Rate out of 10 for how aligned your usage is to your purpose (_ / 10).	___ / 10	__ / 10	__ / 10

*Do you find yourself following less relevant activity such as people's highly curated photos, inflammatory posts, comments on posts that are not relevant, content on other things?

- To what extent are your habits supporting feelings of confidence, relaxation, feeling appropriately informed and being positively connected with others? To what extent are you putting your device down afterwards feeling inspired, happy and fulfilled?

- What one change could you make to your social media habits that would reduce any negative impact on your feelings of happiness and confidence?

Dodging 'death by clubs'

If you sometimes feel overwhelmed by the volume of extracurricular activities you are trying to fit into your children's schedule, it is worth thinking through how much of it is essential and how much is driven by a fear of falling behind and what other people are saying. Is the noise too loud? The logistical matrix of children's clubs and activities can push us to the edge: 'death by clubs'.

Suzy, a senior project manager in more ways than one, was co-ordinating a full schedule of clubs and activities with associated transport each week for her three children. This included football practice, drama class, netball club, swimming club, flute, drums, singing, climbing, sports matches, youth group and Scouts. You get the picture. There is nothing unusual here. I see many of you nodding in recognition.

We all want our children to have access to experiences, opportunities, teamwork, fitness, skills development, camaraderie and friendships. Occasionally, you might hear an honest whisper of 'I can't juggle all of this any more'. We all need to make the decisions that are right for our own families. Maybe it is worth pausing to consider if your own personal version of 'death by clubs' merits a rethink?

Overloading our children is a risk. Research conducted in England with 50 families across 12 primary schools found that 88% of children were participating in organized activities 4 to 5 times a week and 58% were attending more than one activity in a single evening. The research project found this had a detrimental effect on everyone to some degree:

> *'While children might experience some of these benefits, a busy organized activity schedule can put considerable strain on parents' resources and families' relationships, as well as potentially harm children's development and well-being.'*[35]

There is no doubt about it, we are planners, logistics experts and taxi drivers a lot of the week.

Whatever stage of parenting you are at, are you sure what the priority activities are or may there be a combination of FOMO, FOPO and perfectionism at play? It starts early with baby massage, baby music, baby swimming, baby sensory, baby gym and more. Do you look at what other parents are organizing for their children, the achievements other kids make in their sporting, musical, artistic and dramatic endeavours and assume this is what 'good parents' do? For school-aged children, clubs may be a brilliant core solution to childcare requirements; could it be worth checking if you really need to arrange more than that?

We are in danger of organizing our kids (and ourselves) to death. Downtime, playtime, relaxation and recovery are at risk of disappearing when we fall into the trap of exposing

[35] Traci Pederson refers to findings published in *Sport, Education and Society* journal in her 2018 article: https://psychcentral.com/news/2018/05/15/too-many-extracurricular-activities-for-kids-may-do-more-harm-than-good#1

our children to as much stimulation as possible. Maybe you are all happy, relaxed and content juggling your various activities. That's great. If you are not, what can you drop that creates some breathing space for you all?

Nuggets from Chapter 8

- When there are multiple noisy voices telling us what we should do and how to do it, we can be more intentional about who we choose to listen to and why.
- Consider the appreciation ratio in your own communication at work and at home. A small shift from 0:1 or 1:1 up to 2:1 could have a big impact on how motivated others feel.
- Other people's opinions may have value but we are the experts in our own lives; we can turn down the volume and trust our judgement when we have put the thinking time in.
- Social media's benefits come with caveats around our mental health and exposure to unrealistic or irrelevant ideals. Do a mini audit of what you're paying attention to, how long for and how it leaves you feeling. What small changes would be helpful?
- Death by clubs is optional. Review what your family schedule looks like. What is there because it's important and what is there because you're listening to the noise?

9

Thinking traps and how to escape them

As well as filtering the noisy voices around us, we can choose how we listen to our own voice and get to our best quality thinking. In this chapter we will be looking at some of the well-known thinking traps that can be blockers to clear thinking. In Chapter 10, we will do a deeper dive on a loud internal voice that can get in our way: the inner critic.

What are thinking traps?

We know from the Cognitive Triangle in Part 2 that what we *think* is at the root of how we *feel* and how we *behave*. If we want to be really effective, then getting to our best quality thinking is crucial. We can bring back our inner scientist, historian or journalist to mine for the facts and learn how to avoid the thinking traps that lurk around the corner.

Thinking traps, or cognitive distortions, are patterns of thought that get in the way of us seeing things clearly. There are a number of common thinking traps that many of us will recognize. If these play out for you as more than traps you fall into from time to time and seriously interfere with your day-to-day life, it's a good idea to talk to a medical professional.

Common thinking traps

Below are some of the most well-recognized cognitive distortions or thinking traps:

- **All-or-nothing thinking**: things are black and white, perfect or a failure.
- **Magnification or minimization**: making things seem bigger or smaller than they actually are.
- **Filtering**: taking the negative details and inflating them while filtering out the positive things (e.g. you receive one piece of developmental feedback, so you focus on that and forget the seven pieces of positive feedback).
- **Over-generalization**: something happens once and you expect it to happen over and over again (e.g. someone misses a deadline and you never trust them again).
- **Mind-reading**: you assume you know what people are thinking or feeling and why they act the way they

do. (e.g. you assume someone is annoyed with you and seek evidence to prove this is true).

- **Fortune telling**: predicting the future.
- **Catastrophizing**: you expect disaster and assume the worst possible outcome.
- **Personalization**: you think what people do or say is related to you.
- **Control fallacy**: assuming you can control situations.
- **Emotional reasoning**: relying on your emotions rather than logic.
- **Global labelling**: generalizing or stereotyping.
- **Shoulds, oughts, can'ts and musts**: beliefs about what should or can't be done, often stemming from our childhood.

Thinking Trap Bingo

When I introduce thinking traps to clients, it's not unusual for them to identify more than a couple that feel very familiar. Some pull a wry smile and say 'full house'. Don't worry if you spot something similar.

Activity #22: Thinking Trap Bingo

- Place a tick next to all the thinking traps that resonate for you. If you need a reminder, turn back to see the definitions again.

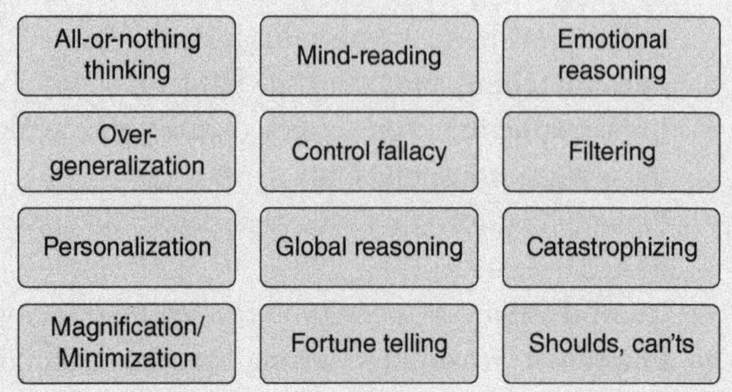

- Draw a star next to the most recognizable one for you.

Think of a time this thinking trap showed up for you recently and reflect on how it got in your way.

If you knew it was a thinking trap, what would have been a more helpful and more balanced thing to think? What would have happened differently if you looked at the situation this way?

Thinking traps in action

Let's return to Sofia, a senior leader who came back to work after adoption leave. Adoption leave is distinctly different from parental leave given the unique emotional journey. The anxiety, hope, disappointments, legalities, logistics and sheer volume of paperwork cannot be underestimated. There was so much for Sofia and her husband to do in this period of parental leave beyond the core business of bonding with and looking after their baby daughter; for the first 9 months they did not know if their daughter would legally be able to remain with them beyond the immediate term. There are adoptive parents who go through all of this and then find they are not able to keep their adopted child which, as Sofia says, is 'beyond heart-breaking'. She reflects:

'For us, the leave was a nightmare because you don't know if you get to keep your child; yet in your eyes and in your heart, they are your child.'

It is so important that managers have a better idea of what is involved for adoptive parents because it is not like other parental leave experiences; adoptive parents return exhausted and vulnerable in a different way.

Sofia returned to work with a BC reputation as a successful leader with a strong work ethic, well-developed people skills, excellent client delivery and impressive commercial results.

She had put clear boundaries around work after returning from adoption leave. She knew these were good decisions for her new family but she was feeling real discomfort. She felt disengaged, she was making harsh assessments of her contribution and she had begun to doubt her value to the firm. There was a sense of loss as well as gain in becoming a Mum as she returned to work. The legacy of her BC expectations of herself at work had tipped over from being motivational to being a pejorative force.

Her thoughts included:

'I am doing a terrible job at work; I think I should quit.'

Thinking traps were getting in her way, particularly catastrophizing, relying on emotional reasoning and filtering.

She was looking at worst-case scenarios (catastrophizing), she was relying on emotion rather than logic (emotional reasoning) and she was ignoring all the positive feedback (filtering). It is easy to feel these extremes when we are in the thick of things, especially when the situation is emotionally charged and we are exhausted.

When Sofia had a chance to slow down and reference her holistic AC success criteria and challenge her thinking traps, she generated helpful and reasonable other thoughts and different ways forward. She set up a meeting with her career advisor to ask for feedback on how things were going.

> *'I had no real evidence that I was doing a terrible job. In fact, people were saying the opposite. I was leading the team well. The consulting market was tough for everyone at that point; my commercial results were no worse than anyone else's. It was my own expectations of myself that led me to think I was letting people down.'*

Across her own personal performance matrix, Sofia was achieving a great deal. She had taken a step back from some things that she would have taken on at work in the BC era to prioritize time with her child, but she was not underperforming. She was performing across the big picture of her life. She was able to hold back the pressing boulder of self-expectation enough to see the need for some grace and space for herself. She pressed pause on writing that letter of resignation.

When I caught up with Sofia 12 months later to see what things were like for her now, she had this honest response:

> *'I'm ruthless with my diary. I do less, both fun and work. It's the honest view. I do less but I think I do more of the*

important stuff. I have time with my daughter. I have help in the house where it is possible.

Completely unexpectedly, I take joy in the rare business trips which I had initially been dreading. I can take the team out for dinner, I eat an adult dinner as opposed to leftover nursery food and I sit down and talk uninterrupted. I sleep uninterrupted, which I didn't think my body would remember how to do. But it does!'

Nuggets from Chapter 9

- We all fall into thinking traps; they are common distortions. When we have a name for them and are aware of them, it is easier to spot what's happening in our thinking.
- Play Thinking Trap Bingo: how many feel like common traps for you? If you know that, how can you be more conscious of these patterns?
- Rather than feeling hemmed in by thinking traps, communicate with trusted others to get a fresh perspective on the situation. Test out if they see it the same way.
- Challenge yourself to step into the opposite frame of mind from the thinking trap you're grappling with. For example, if you know you catastrophize, spend a minute thinking about the issue as an optimist and see what comes out.

10

Your inner critic and how to befriend it

Let's (not) talk about imposter syndrome

One of the noisiest voices we need to apply selective listening to is the inner narrative that tells us we're not enough. Firstly, let's get our terminology into a more helpful frame. You may have heard of or referenced 'imposter syndrome' when talking about yourself feeling a bit of a fraud at work, or a colleague believing deep down they are not good enough. It's a phrase that's used a lot. We can make an important and potentially far healthier shift to how we think and talk about the voice of self-doubt that so many of us recognize.

Let's put the idea of a syndrome to one side. Clance and Imes originally coined the phrase 'imposter phenomenon' rather than 'imposter syndrome' in their 1978 article focused on a study of high-achieving women.[36] It has been taken out of context since then. The word 'syndrome' implies a disease or disorder; a set of medical symptoms that may join up to indicate illness. Whilst recognizing there will be cases where thought patterns are significantly affecting mental health and seeing a medical professional is the right thing to do,

[36] Pauline Rose Clance and Suzanne Imes, 'The Imposter Phenomenon in High Achieving Women: Dynamics and Therapeutic Intervention', 1978.

it's not the case for the majority of people. You are not ill if you sometimes feel a sense of self-doubt, particularly when you're under pressure, but you can find new ways to get into more effective thinking patterns much more quickly that will be more helpful to you when you feel the doubt take over.

Let's talk about the inner critic

Do you recognize the voice that tells you 'it's not going to work', 'you'll get found out' or 'you're going to fail'? Or perhaps 'others are better than you', 'keep your head down' or 'work harder'? We can refer to this narrative as the inner critic.

Amy, a journalist, Mum of two and Stepmum of one, says:

> *'I struggle to give myself permission to rest. It is something I find really difficult even at the weekend. I am telling myself before I sit down that I have not earnt my time to stop.'*

These critical thoughts are not intrinsically bad. For example, they may spur you on to persevere, to work hard and commit to things. Many working parents would agree that this voice may be harsh but it's part of the reason they are successful and so motivated. At what point does the voice begin to be unhelpful and counterproductive? Inevitably, strengths get overplayed. If the thinking is so powerful that it prevents you from making a change you really want to make or from being sustainably healthy it merits closer attention.

The good news is, you can find new ways to ensure you get more quickly into more effective thinking patterns that will be helpful to you. The unsurprising news is that there is no magic wand and it will take some effort on your part. But let me offer more good news here: even a bit of practice can make a significant difference.

The inner critic can be on overdrive, identifying threats where there may be none, and getting louder than it should be. It stops being helpful because it's reacting to something that may go a long way back or it's being triggered by an experience that is no longer relevant. It's an easy-to-access, well-trodden route of thought that's familiar and quick to follow. It's an emotional response, faster than the more logical thinking our brain is also capable of, because it is all about keeping us safe.

When is a tiger not a tiger?

Think of our ancestors who, once upon a time, would have been on the lookout for a large predator in their daily life. For most of us in the modern world, this is less of a concern. But imagine, for a moment, that a tiger leapt out of a bush in front of you. In this situation, the brain needs to be lightning quick to process the danger that has emerged and get ready in a split second to respond. We don't want to hang around, trying to evaluate if this truly is something we ought to be concerned about. We prepare to fight the danger, run away or freeze.

It is known as the flight-fight-freeze response. The amygdala, part of the limbic system responsible for processing emotions, particularly fear, is designed to operate in this way to keep you safe. You'll know what this feels like in your body when something suddenly makes you jump. Your heart rate increases, your breath gets shallower, you feel pumped. Your physiology has changed because a danger has been detected and you need to be ready for action.

When we feel threatened our amygdala, the threat detector, 'acts as a storehouse of emotional memory'[37] and can be remembering previous situations where we have not felt safe. These can be major or minor in nature. For major issues where there is trauma present, the best place to explore these safely is by talking to a medical professional or therapist. In the majority of cases, the situations are significant to us but are not in the realm of trauma. For example, situations at work where we got negative responses or felt rejected or childhood experiences of exclusion. Our inner critic remembers these and wants to keep us away from risky experiences.

This holds us back because it's dominating our responses and not allowing the longer-term, rational decision-making part of our brain to put forward alternative points of view. We find we have a kind of tunnel vision, and an echo chamber based on the most fearful part of ourselves. We lack quick access to the more balanced perspectives that are also present and need to be listened to if we are to move forward effectively.

For some, the inner critic is very well developed and has a harsh and destructive voice. It's a saboteur. It's important to separate out what the helpful grain of truth about risk is and what's no longer relevant to us as adults in this moment. It can help to depersonalize the critic so that we recognize it as the voice of only the risks or the negatives rather than the entirety of 'you'.

[37] Daniel Goleman, *Emotional Intelligence: Why It Can Matter More Than IQ*, 1996, p. 15. If you are interested to read further, Goleman explains the emotional brain and the role of the amygdala on pp. 15–29.

Getting to know your inner critic

You can get to know how the inner critic speaks, the tone of voice, the kinds of things it says and when it gets loudest. If you understand more about it, you are better able to recognize when it is loud and this introduces more choice about how much air time you give it.

I'd like to introduce you to a useful tool: the ABCDE framework.[38]

ABCDE helps us identify what the inner critic is saying, the effect it has and how to develop more helpful thinking. You can find an identity for the inner critic's voice, which helps you create more space between you and it. As one of my clients coined it, her inner critic is 'a combination of past voices that are not really me'. Another worked through ABCDE, hearing the inner critic out loud for the first time, and instantly recognized the voice of a critical parent.

A few working parents shared their experiences of the inner critic:

- A voice that tells me I am not allowed to have a rest or sit down because that would be lazy.
- A voice that says holiday should only be used for something big like going away.
- A voice that believes I don't deserve to be at the boardroom table with senior leaders because I don't have enough to say.

[38] ABCDE was developed by Albert Ellis, an American psychologist and psychotherapist who founded rational-emotive behaviour therapy in the twentieth century. ABCDE is often used today in cognitive behavioural therapy and it's successfully made the jump to being relevant in the field of coaching.

- A voice that tells me I will stumble and make a fool of myself if I stand up to give a talk to a group.
- A voice that says I don't know enough to go for a new role.

Befriending the inner critic is possible through recognizing the role it's playing, realizing where it comes from, what happens to our bodies and behaviours when it's active and creating new neural pathways to access different thinking more quickly. It's less about trying to eradicate the voice of the inner critic and, rather, acknowledging its presence, thanking it for the warning but quickly putting our energy into calming the system down and having good strategies to access more effective thinking. We are recategorizing things from 'tiger' to something much less threatening.

As easy as ABCDE

There are two stages:

ABC: *getting to know exactly what your inner critic is saying* and what happens in your body as a result, so you will be more able to recognize when the inner critic is at work.

DE: *developing truer and more helpful thinking* that will serve you better.

Activity #23 invites you to try out ABCDE. The framework is explained below to help you understand what each step is about before you begin.

	What?	Think about…	Write down…
A	Activating event	What is the situation or trigger that fires up your inner critic?	Where were you? Who were you with? What was happening?
B	Beliefs	What do you believe is true at this moment of activation? What are you saying to yourself about you? What are you saying to yourself that others may think?	Be forensic about the statements in your head. If we were able to listen in to the inner narrative, what might we hear you saying to yourself in that moment? For example, 'I am not as good at this as others…', 'I am not expert enough', 'Others think I'm stupid'. Notice the tone of voice too.
C	Consequences	What's happening in your body and to your behaviour?	In that moment what would you notice in physiological terms? (That is, what is happening in your body?)

	What?	Think about…	Write down…
			Heart rate? Breathing? Tension spots in your body? Posture? Externally: What might others notice? (For example, withdrawal, going quiet or getting louder, being defensive.)
D	**D**isputing statements	Now you have more distance from that moment… What is both *truer and more helpful* to say to yourself than the statements in B?	Read aloud each of your B statements. For each one, write something truer and more helpful. If this is hard to do, imagine what a trusted and reliable supporter of yours might say if we asked them to give an answer.

	What?	Think about…	Write down…
E	Effective thinking	Which of these D thought(s) can you connect to most easily and begin to access more frequently?	Pick one or two D statements that feel the most powerful and relevant to you. Write them down and keep them near your workspace. Practise saying them out loud and simultaneously breathing slowly and deeply. Spend time with them daily.

Activity #23: ABCDE

- Work through the ABCDE table slowly and forensically. It is most powerful when we pinpoint exactly what we are thinking and feeling at each stage.
- After this, consider how your 'B voice' makes you feel. Write down adjectives that describe those feelings.
- Can you give this 'B voice' a label? For example, an adjective that encapsulates its tone and nature, or a character it reminds you

of, or a person in your life? A few examples from clients: Gloom-fest, one of the Muppets, a parent's name, a piano teacher's name, Angry Barry, The Undermining Voice, The Judge, Anti-Me.

- Now listen to the voice in section D and notice how it makes you feel. Can you give it a label like you did for your 'B voice' above? A few examples: Real Me, a good friend's name, an encouraging parent's name, Sunshine Voice, The Fair Voice, Logical Me, The Empowering Voice.

Having a shorthand meaningful label for the 'B voice' (the inner critic) helps you acknowledge it and thank it for showing up to keep you safe. Then ask your 'D voice' for some input. Naming your 'D voice' meaningfully is a great start to connecting more closely with alternative thoughts and getting quicker access to them. Is your 'D voice' the name of a supportive friend or relative? Is it you as a manager of others, able to offer the kind of support that's needed in difficult moments? Is it you in a state of flow when you feel that surge of assurance and belief about your abilities?

A further suggestion to deepen your emotional connection with those more helpful thoughts is to find an image that represents your 'D voice':

- Where in your life have you most embodied the spirit of your 'D voice'? Have a think about when and where you feel balanced, fair on yourself and most positive? Is it with family, travelling, on the sports pitch, in a particular role or phase of your life?

- Find a photo that encapsulates you feeling and behaving more in line with this version of you. Or is there an image that encapsulates the spirit of your 'D voice'? For example, one client found an image of the mountains helped her get to her 'D voice' quickly. Perhaps it's you as a manager, where you are able to offer compassion and empathy to others and operate from this place of understanding and care?
- Print it out and have it on your wall near your workspace at home or in your notebook or bag if you are on the move. Pair it with the name of your 'D voice' and one or two of the most powerful D statements you identified in ABCDE. Look at this regularly, not just when you feel the inner critic get louder.

The more you create an emotional connection to the new voice you've developed, the easier it will be to access this version of your thinking when you most need it. And just like strengthening muscles in the gym, practising thinking and feeling that way will build strength in accessing your most effective thinking (i.e. deepening the new neural pathways you've been creating).

Laura named her inner critic after a particularly critical childhood teacher. She found it useful to greet Mrs K., recognize that was who was talking, thank her for trying to keep her sharp and then invite her more balanced and supportive 'D voice' to think and speak.

Emma stepped into her manager mode to find her 'D voice'. Reconnecting to this compassionate version of herself when dealing with team members and her genuine belief as a manager that time away was vital for others, helped her to challenge a 'B voice' which was saying taking time off was wrong. What would she say to a direct report if she heard them say this? What would her compassionate manager self ('D voice') have to say?

Kayode was a successful senior manager and father of two, viewed by his firm as someone with the potential to be promoted to the next step. He would need to focus more on the commercial side of his role, having more sales conversations, but felt an almost nauseating sense of fear when faced with the prospect of presenting himself as an *expert* to potential new clients he had not already 'proven his worth' to.

For Kayode, the inner critic had grown in volume a long time ago at university where he felt, erroneously, that he was 'averagely intelligent' compared to peers. This was one of the best universities in the world. He learnt to keep his head down and developed a silent sense of inferiority. He therefore stepped away from situations where he might be perceived as setting himself up as an expert or might get 'found out'. He needed to acknowledge that his inner critic was trying to keep him safe but that it was outdated and inaccurate. His 'D voice' knew he had genuine expertise and the opportunity to bring that to new clients. His firm needed to see his belief in this too.

You can make changes to your thinking habits. You can befriend the inner critic. Give your 'D voice' some more regular airtime and notice what changes.

And breathe...

Breathing is the most overlooked tool in our toolkit. It sounds so simple that we often don't give it enough credence. The Navy Seals famously use box breathing before a mission to ensure they calm their systems down to access their most logical and rational thinking: it is that effective. As we discovered earlier, the amygdala is primed to respond instinctively to a sense of threat. Our breathing becomes shallow, our heart rate is raised and our thoughts are emotional and less rational. In other words, your body is doing what your brain tells it to do.

When you notice your inner critic at work, Step 1 is to calm this response. The quickest way to better thinking is to shift your physiological state first: breathing is your go-to technique. Box breathing is simple, and even in the space of a minute or two you will notice a significant shift in your physiology and state of mind.

It might be useful to consider box-breathing exercises for your children when they are anxious too. There are simple, colourful videos on YouTube, such as watching a fish swim around a 4-sided box or watching a shape expand and contract in time with the breaths.[39] Kids find them easy to follow. They're not bad for adults too!

[39] Triangle breathing from The Mindfulness Teacher: Holly Morris, 2021, www.youtube.com/watch?v=RpI9bm3lTQw

Activity #24: Box breathing

Imagine a box or a square. It has 4 sides and you are going to move along each side of the box to the count of 4 as you breathe:

- Breathe in through your nose for a count of 4 as you move along one side of the box.
- Hold that breath for a count of 4 as you move along the next side of the box.
- Breathe out of your mouth for a count of 4 as you move along the third side of the box.
- Hold that breath for the count of 4 along the final side of the box.
- Repeat a few times before returning to breathing normally.

Notice how you feel calmer and more present. It's something you can do any time, even in company, without it being too obvious. If you can firstly get your body into a calmer state, you will be able to summon your 'D voice' more easily.

Nuggets from Chapter 10

- Consider ditching 'imposter syndrome' and talking instead about your inner critic: there is not something wrong with you if you notice self-doubt.
- The inner critic is trying to help by keeping you safe. You can reframe what seems dangerous to something less threatening and unlock calmer responses.
- Get to know your inner critic using ABCDE. Name your 'B voice'. Name your 'D voice' and attach an image to it that resonates.
- Spend time with your 'D voice', read its true and helpful statements often and practise asking it to share a view when you feel the rise of the inner critic.
- Breathe. Try out box breathing for 1 minute and notice the change in your physiology and increased ability to access your 'D voice'.

Part 5

Getting unstuck

'Iterating into the right solution for your particular equation is part of the process. Never see it as a failure but the road to arriving at the best solutions.'

(Marga, senior engineer, Formula 1)

11

All the feelings

Everyone has emotions

It's not unusual to feel overwhelmed by emotion sometimes. Working parents have more than their fair share of feelings to absorb and process. There are our own emotions, generated by the multiple dimensions of our lives and then there are those of our family too. For example, emotions hit us hard when our children are struggling or expressing unhappiness, sadness or anxiety. We worry, empathize and do our best to help.

Emotions are part of being human, although there is still cultural hesitancy in acknowledging this is as true for men as it is for women. Dom remembers reading a book before becoming a father which he terms a 'Commando Dad'-style parenting book. It felt like an army manual for new Dads focused on practical matters, such as how to change a nappy in three rapid steps. It was useful but there was a noticeable absence of recognition of the complex emotions one feels on becoming a father and beyond. Emotions often seem to find a more natural home in resources for mothers but as Dom puts it, 'Dads have emotions too!'

Getting stuck in emotion

It may feel we have one of two options: suppress emotion in order to keep calm and carry on or let emotion swamp us and render us immobile. Susan David, a Harvard psychologist, has developed the idea of emotional agility, which she defines as the ability to be with your emotions with openness, curiosity and compassion. Her research finds people often respond to difficult emotions by either *bottling* (suppressing or ignoring them) or *brooding* (ruminating or getting stuck). Both responses, she found, predict higher levels of anxiety, depression and burnout. Instead, David advocates for recognizing emotions accurately ('naming them'), accepting them without judgement, and using them as data, not directives, to guide thoughtful action. This flexibility has been linked to greater wellbeing, better performance and improved relationships.

Labelling emotions

Maddie was sitting on the floor one night wondering what to do with herself. She felt empty and full at the same time. Empty because it really did feel like she had nothing left to give and full because she was overwhelmed with feelings. That's when she spotted the bright pink notepad her child had left by her bed. Maddie had read about writing down feelings as a helpful way to clear the mind before bed but had never tried it.

In a moment of inspiration or desperation, she opened the notepad and began to write down adjectives to describe how she was feeling. She started by writing down just the words 'sad' and 'anxious' in the middle of a page. That's all she thought she felt. When she pushed herself a bit more to consider what else she was feeling she added 'alone' and 'frustrated'... and 'exposed' and 'vulnerable'. In fact, more specifically, 'scared'.

Interestingly, Maddie noticed that once she had acknowledged the weighty, dense emotions on the page and identified the presence of 'scared', she did feel a bit lighter and discovered some other things she was feeling that she didn't know were there. She realized she also felt 'optimistic' about some things and 'grateful' for quite a few things. In fact, she felt a lot of positives but they had been buried under the heaviness of all the previously unarticulated emotions. They were all equally important but it had been hard to see some of them. She could take action to reduce the fear she felt about a situation at work, and there were other feelings to discover too.

Labelling your emotions is a helpful exercise whatever time of day you decide to do it, because it's an expedient route to feeling different, faster. It can be particularly helpful before bed so that we clear the mind ready for sleep.

The Wheel of Emotions

The Wheel of Emotions[40] is a helpful tool in identifying specific emotions. It's a way of getting granular about what we are feeling. There are a number of versions of the wheel; I've picked one to share here and invite you to explore it in the next activity.

[40] The Wheel of Emotions is based on the work of American psychologist Robert Plutchik and The Feelings Wheel developed by Dr Gloria Wilcox. See for example, *The Feelings Wheel: Unlock the Power of Your Emotions*, 2025, www.calm.com/blog/the-feelings-wheel

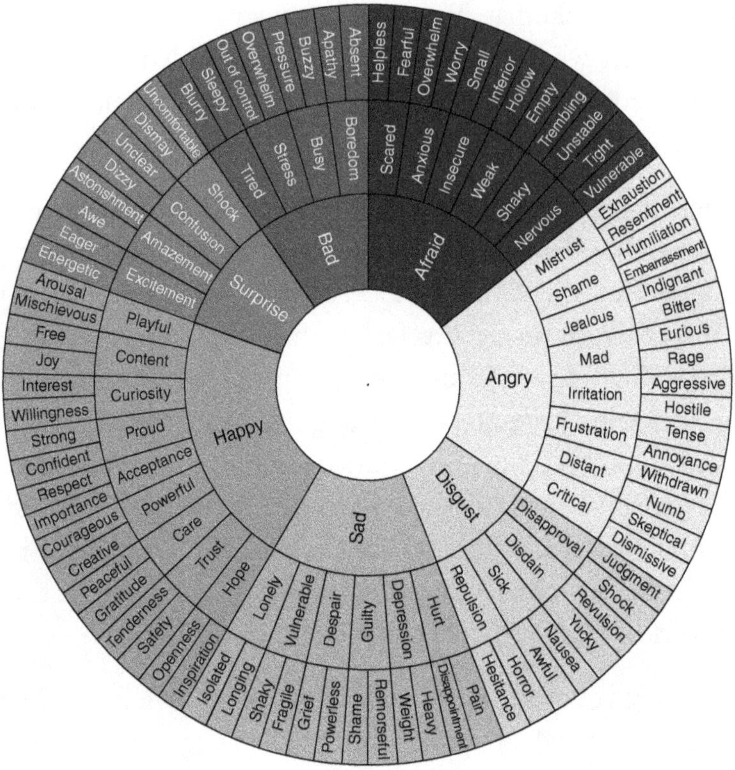

Afraid
Scared — Helpless, Fearful
Anxious — Overwhelm, Worry
Insecure — Small, Inferior
Weak — Hollow, Empty
Shaky — Trembling, Unstable
Nervous — Tight, Vulnerable

Angry
Mistrust — Exhaustion, Resentment
Shame — Humiliation, Embarrassment
Jealous — Indignant, Bitter
Mad — Furious, Rage
Irritation — Aggressive, Hostile
Frustration — Tense, Annoyance

Disgust
Distant — Withdrawn, Numb
Critical — Skeptical, Dismissive
Disapproval — Judgment, Shock
Disdain — Revulsion, Yucky
Sick — Nausea, Awful
Repulsion — Horror, Hesitance

Sad
Hurt — Pain, Disappointment
Depression — Heavy, Weight
Guilty — Remorseful, Shame
Despair — Powerless, Grief
Vulnerable — Fragile, Shaky
Lonely — Longing, Isolated

Happy
Hope — Inspiration, Openness
Trust — Safety, Tenderness
Care — Gratitude, Peaceful
Powerful — Creative, Courageous
Acceptance — Importance, Respect
Proud — Confident, Strong
Curiosity — Willingness, Interest
Content — Joy, Free
Playful — Mischievous, Arousal

Surprise
Excitement — Energetic, Eager
Amazement — Awe, Astonishment
Confusion — Dizzy, Unclear
Shock — Dismay, Uncomfortable

Bad
Tired — Blurry, Sleepy
Stress — Out of control, Overwhelm
Busy — Pressure, Buzzy
Boredom — Apathy, Absent

Activity #25: The Wheel of Emotions

- Start in the centre of the wheel. Consider which primary emotions reflect what you are feeling at this moment.
- Write down the most significant emotions you notice first. For example, sad. Acknowledge it.
- From there, work outwards. For example, you may feel a top line sense of sadness and

when you dig below that, perhaps the more accurate label is that you feel lonely. And maybe when you think about it, the more specific feeling is that you feel isolated. Find the emotions that really resonate most with how you are feeling as you work outwards through the wheel. Acknowledge them.

- Write your emotions on a piece of paper, in your journal or wherever is going to be most appropriate for you. Physically writing the words makes a difference.
- There is no 'right answer'; you won't be wrong. It expands your awareness and literacy of what the emotions are, allowing you to feel them and give them accurate labels.
- As you write down the most prominent feelings, take a look at other aspects of the wheel that you may not yet have focused on. Are there any feelings you notice that have been hiding? Might there be an element of 'hopeful' or 'courageous', for example?

The Wheel of Emotions is a guide to help you get started. You will find you become more articulate at labelling your emotions after a while and you can follow your own track. Making a scan of The Wheel of Emotions part of your ready-for-bed routine or your commute as you decompress from work and transition to home can be really helpful.

Recognizing emotions can be challenging. Identifying emotions can be especially difficult for those of us who may have diagnosed or undiagnosed autism.

Simon, a partner in a firm with two young children, had always noticed he struggled to identify emotions in himself and others. Around 5 years ago he was diagnosed with autism, prosopagnosia (face blindness) and alexithymia (difficulty experiencing and identifying emotions). Simon has found The Wheel of Emotions to be a useful tool in coaching sessions and in an everyday way. He has been learning to categorize a wider range of emotions for himself and to recognize them more in others.

It is 'hard work', as he puts it, as it requires a significant degree of mental energy but he has found it helpful at work and at home. He reflects that the alexithymia has been a source of real challenge at points in his career. It has sometimes got in the way of relationships and communication at work: he has 'got things wrong and had to apologize', in his words. The granularity of the Wheel of Emotions supports him in understanding emotion and applying this understanding to himself and others around him. With some discipline and practice, emotions now feel more differentiated and Simon is able to apply this in a way that supports his wellbeing and his effectiveness. We all can.

Beyond 'think positive'

There is real strength in being able to channel positive thoughts and feelings. However, just to adopt a mantra of 'think positive' is rarely effective. Forced positivity can be toxic. Pretending we aren't feeling sad or worried, for example, is not helpful to us. Many of us grew up believing we just needed to get a grip and get on. We can believe emotional signals should be ignored, overridden or are unhelpful if we have grown up in a system where this is what the role models tell or show us. We may think resilience is not letting the feelings be felt and that grit means pushing emotion out of the way.

However, healthy resilience is intimately connected to our degree of emotional literacy. Understanding what we are feeling and why and developing effective ways to move through emotions can make a huge difference to how we think, feel and behave. This has a significant impact not only on ourselves but on those around us at work and at home. It's about being well. It's about productivity, efficiency and effectiveness. It's about great leadership. Being aware of and regulating the emotional shadow we cast has real impact on our teams, clients, peers and family. It influences the extent to which we can help others be at their best. It's a fantastic skill for managers to develop. We can make intentional choices about how we respond to emotion more of the time.

Developing emotional agility

Emotion is not to be feared. Some of us try to squash emotion or find it difficult to be conscious of what we are really feeling. For others, emotion runs close to the surface and tears can come easily as a way of physically expressing a range of emotions, not necessarily sadness.

Emotional avoidance cuts us off from joy, empathy and connection. We can learn how to move through emotions, rather than feeling stuck in them or trying to move around them. The results are improved self-regulation, better mental health and greater resilience generating grounded, value-driven parenting and professional leadership. Your feelings aren't flaws; they're signals. Listen first, act second.

This next activity is derived from the work of Susan David and Brené Brown. It's a short exercise to help you get granular about your emotions, work out what's really at the root of the feelings, choose how to react and then reset. It's about helping you see emotions as 'data, not directives', as David puts it, and lessening shame, as Brown highlights.[41] As we have seen, getting specific about your emotions increases resilience and enables more intentional responses.

Activity #26: Developing emotional agility for better outcomes

Ask yourself, 'What am I feeling?' Take a few deep breaths, close your eyes and notice sensations in your body. Is it tension? Unease? What else?

- **Name** the emotions you are feeling. Get specific and use the Wheel of Emotions in Activity #25 (e.g. instead of 'stressed', try to be more granular. Is it 'overwhelmed'?)
- **Acknowledge** it: say to yourself: 'I'm noticing X emotion. I'll let it be without pushing it away.'

[41] Susan David, 2022, www.susandavid.com/newsletter/recognizing-your-emotions-as-data-not-directives/; Brené Brown, *Dare to Lead*.

- **Listen** to what signal it is giving you. Emotion is data (e.g. 'I'm feeling resentful. What is this trying to tell me? What value of mine might be getting squashed, making me feel that way?')
- **Respond.** Choose one of these actions:
    - Accept it ('It's OK that I feel this').
    - Share it ('I'm feeling let down. Can we talk about it?').
    - Set a boundary ('I need 20 mins by myself after work today').
    - Shift with kindness ('I'm disappointed but I'll show up gently').

As working parents, we create margin for ourselves when we take a step back and create a space before we respond. And it is imperative we find ways to lessen emotional stress for our long-term health. The more effectively we work with our emotions, the less anxious and stressed we will feel. The mind-body connection is well documented. There is no doubt that stress impacts our health. Developing emotional agility is important to our wellbeing and makes us better parents, partners, leaders and colleagues.

Nuggets from Chapter 11

- Emotions are not to be feared and send us important information that we can pay attention to.
- Labelling emotions is a powerful way to increase awareness of what you are feeling and to get specific about it. Try out the Wheel of Emotions to help you identify emotions.
- The degree to which you are aware of your emotions and are able to self-regulate has a significant impact on your leadership shadow at work and at home.
- Emotional agility is more effective than a binary 'think positive' approach: when we acknowledge emotions we can choose how to respond, reset and move forward more quickly.

12

Career smarts

Chapters and seasons

As working parents, it can feel like we are constantly making big decisions about whether to drive forward with our career, stay where we are or take a step back to create margin in the madness.

There are different chapters in our working lives where we may be pushing on with progression, maintaining the career status quo or scaling back; we can look at these as seasons rather than a permanent state of affairs. I don't buy into the myth that 6–12 months, or even longer, of maintaining or scaling back has a material impact on our long-term careers. It's an understandable concern for those of us in professions where promotions happen every couple of years and the peer ladder is highly visible. Even so, a short chapter taking longer at a current career level while we are in the most logistically and physically demanding stage of parenthood means we may be more sustainably successful in the long run.

Marga is a senior engineer in Formula 1 motorsport and as one of the very few women in her industry she is used to constantly breaking new ground in her career. She is one of the only women to have stood on the podium at a Grand Prix, recognized for her vital role in the trackside team, and has been instrumental to the success of her team. When she returned from maternity leave (one of the few engineers to have a maternity leave) she moved from trackside to the factory team. Travelling the world many months of the year with the team was not how she wanted early parenthood to be but she was no less passionate about her work. She requested an adjusted work pattern to accommodate nursery timings and proper time with her child in the evenings.

Marga is in no doubt about her priorities: her baby comes first. However, there were naturally challenges in leaving the trackside team, learning a new role, managing teams of engineers and balancing a demanding job with parenting. Whilst it was a big adjustment, she reflects on how this shift has widened her understanding of the whole picture: she brings invaluable first-hand trackside knowledge to the factory and, if and when she returns trackside, she will be better for the insight she now has. The new role is opening up different aspects of the industry she loves and rather than slowing her down, she realizes it's widened her scope for diverse and more senior roles. In summary, rather than stepping back, the step she took was both upwards to management and sideways to the factory team and she has combined this successfully with motherhood. Once again, she is trailblazing and opening up the path for women who may follow behind her.

We can't always know how it is going to turn out. If you're just back to work after parental leave, your current thoughts are not going to be the same as in 6 months' time. Take a breath and allow time for adjustment. If you're further into the juggle, maybe you're considering what's next. We can get stuck in a way of looking at things owing to limited time to think or assumptions about what's possible. We can try out the game-changing thinking from earlier in the book and, simultaneously, judiciously choose to listen to people we trust. We need not be alone.

Resourcing for success

Everyone needs support. Getting strategic about how we access this can make a big difference to how resourced and balanced we feel, especially when it comes to careers. Having the right people in our networks can make all the difference to how we view, decide and action our career steps, whether that's upwards, outwards or sideways. I love Tupper and Ellis' concept of the 'squiggly career'. As they point out, seeing your career as a ladder is not helpful. It's a new era of work, careers are less linear and more unpredictable, and ways of working are changing.[42] We can sit in the driving seat of our careers and a key element is building a network that works for you.

Recruiting your Circle of Support

It is one of the easiest things to drop when your life is crammed with commitments. Before you had children you may have had multiple catch-ups with old bosses, mentors, current managers, advocates, recruitment specialists, professional and personal friends and more. Maybe you still have a few

[42] Helen Tupper and Sarah Ellis, *The Squiggly Career: Ditch the Ladder, Discover Opportunity, Design your Career*, 2024.

trusted people you talk to about career decisions. Have you thought about the full range of roles you need to fill to create your optimum career Circle of Support?

When we are short of time for social meet-ups or catch-up meetings, getting specific and intentional about key roles you need to fill in your Circle of Support helps you make the most effective use of time and energy and hopefully brings enjoyable connection too. It's reciprocal: you will be giving as well as receiving.

Getting intentional means you can focus and prioritize your time where the most relevant support can be found, ensuring there is diversity in the opinions you hear and the type of conversations we have. For example, avoiding the pitfall of repeatedly sourcing emotional support in the time you have available to you whilst overlooking the benefit a more formal work champion could bring. Getting strategic about your support network is vital whatever your career focus.

It's sometimes referred to as creating your own Board of Directors, where you appoint people to advise you much like a business might. Whether the concept of recruiting your Board or your Circle of Support resonates more, go with it. I've chosen the Circle of Support here.

7 key roles

These 7 key roles need filling to resource you with career conversations, good thinking, connections and sound counsel.

1. **Coach** (not necessarily a professional one; someone who listens and asks you brilliant questions that really make you think).

In short, this is a person who is excellent at listening, creating enough space for you to think and asking really good questions. Avoid someone who tends to do most of the talking, tells you what you should do or who shares their own experiences as a default mode. (You can source this kind of support in another role such as a mentor.) It's someone who makes you feel heard, offers generous listening and is curious to help you find out what's going on in your own thinking.

2. **Cheerleader** (your biggest fan, they have your back, they offer that shot of positivity when it seems hard to find).
   Once you stop to recognize this as a role in your informal network, hopefully you will find it easy to name the person or people who support you in this way. It's someone who knows your strengths and reminds you that quite frankly you're a superstar. Notice that if you want to caveat this by saying they are partial and biased, you really need this person. The fact that they are positive does not relegate their contribution to invalidity, quite the opposite.
3. **Connector** (they know everyone and, if they don't know a person they probably know someone who does. Natural relationship builders, well-networked and outward-looking).
   It's the person who enjoys meeting new people and is curious to find out what they do. Maybe they are prolific on LinkedIn or are often found having coffee chats with old and new connections. They have their ear to the ground and value building and maintaining their network. You might want two people in this role: one internal to your workplace who is really

well networked in your organization and one external connector in the world beyond your place of work. A connector can make introductions to key people you would benefit from meeting. They act as a bridge to others who know about the thing you need to learn or can help you expand your network for visibility, reciprocal relationships and new opportunities.

4. **Collaborator** (solid peer; you often end up working on things together, great at additive and productive 'test-and-learn' thinking).
   This is someone you work well with and there is an ease to your collaboration. They are open to hearing your ideas and build on them generously. This is a person who you can take a knotty work issue to, or a new concept, and know they will help you work through it, maybe doing some test and learn along the way with you.
5. **Counsellor** (not necessarily a professional one: a person who is there for you when you need to share what's really on your heart and mind).
   They are the person you can open up to and they are ok with you showing emotion and vulnerability. They offer confidentiality and compassion, a safe place to rant, cry and laugh. They allow you to speak freely and honestly about what's really going on and the impact it is having on you.
6. **Champion** (different from the cheerleader; someone who is both willing and able to sponsor your career).
   This is the person who can name you in the right kind of meetings, sing your praises with the right people and who puts forward the case for you and whatever you are focused on achieving next in your career.

7. **Critical friend** (not necessarily a close friend; someone you trust to be honest and challenge your thinking in a helpful way).

   You don't necessarily go to them for emotional support, but you choose to talk to them because they say it like it is and help you see clearly even when this may at times feel hard. This doesn't need to be someone who is blunt or harsh; some people have the gift of offering critical thinking gently and compassionately. It needs to be someone you respect and listen to even when the message is not easy to receive.

A reason, a season or a lifetime

Consider the suitability and usefulness of the people you need in each of the roles. It's ok to have some close friends and family in the network but notice if they are all in that category and ask yourself if it would be useful to look beyond this group. You're looking for the most balanced and relevant perspectives.

Emma, a marketing director, has found it helpful to switch people in and out of her circle as life has progressed. She quotes the poet, Brian A. 'Drew' Chalker:

'People come into your life for a reason, a season or a lifetime.'

Some will come and go and others will be there for the long term. It's OK for some of your circle to be there for a particular reason or a period of your life. For Emma, a previous MD is a lifetime circle member, MBA colleagues have taken up circle roles for a period and then less so, a former boss was key until retirement and university friends are lifelong members of her circle.

Activity #27: Recruiting your Circle of Support

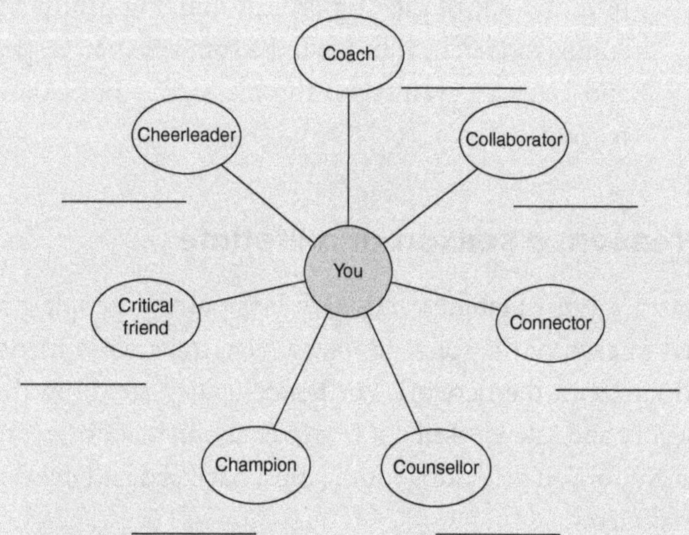

- Firstly, identify where you already have roles filled but perhaps didn't realize it. Write down names next to the bubbles.
- Then identify the gaps where you need someone to operate in that capacity for you. Mark these bubbles with a question mark.
- Refer back to the seven role descriptions above to ensure you are looking for the most

relevant qualities. Who can you ask to fulfil that role? Who do you know who might be able to recommend someone who could fill that role for you and make an introduction?

- Think about the diversity of experience, thought, approach and background that will be most helpful across all the roles in your Circle of Support.

Putting the Circle of Support into practice

Once you have identified who you would like in your Circle of Support, you can set out a pattern of when and why you want to spend time with them. Who do you want a coffee or meeting with over the next 6 months? Prioritize whose perspective you want to tap into.

Over the course of a year, consider what's a reasonable pattern. Whilst you may meet with a couple of them once a year, others may be every 6 months. Some you will talk to more frequently if they naturally cross over into your work schedule or friendships, such as the Collaborator and the Cheerleader.

It may sound a lot of people to maintain relationships with but it is fluid. Maybe at certain points your Champion needs to be more in the loop on what you want next in your career: they need to know what your wins have been so that they can shout about them and introduce your name in the right forums. Others will be on an ad hoc basis with spontaneous get-togethers.

One approach is to analyse which of the roles you will be less likely to turn to as part of your natural rhythm. These are the ones with whom you want to book in a couple of markers in the diary for a catch-up, so you don't forget to draw on them.

A strategic review of where you are spending your time and who you are talking to can only benefit your career. Managers can support their team to think more about this too. When time is the resource you struggle most to conjure, the effectiveness of knowing who you need to talk to and when makes a difference. Clearly, there can be some excellent cross-over between friends and work within your Circle of Support. Recruiting people who are a couple of steps ahead of you on whatever path you are trying to master can be really helpful. For example, if you're weighing up a career move, speaking with parents whose children are a little bit older than yours can help get perspective and give you the confidence that it *is* possible.

Nuggets from Chapter 12

- Look at your career as a series of chapters and seasons: periods of maintaining the status quo, scaling back and acceleration are all part of it. One short period does not define your career.
- New opportunities emerge from sideways steps and a squiggly approach to careers.
- Protecting your priorities does not equal career suicide.
- Recruit a Circle of Support to resource your career: fill seven key roles for balanced and diverse support. Go wider than you might normally to seek different perspectives.
- Review and revitalize your Circle of Support as things evolve: roles may be for a season, a reason or a lifetime.

13

Maps to get you moving

Whether at work or at home, it can be easy to feel cornered in a situation or stuck and unsure how to move forward. These aren't always huge issues or major decisions: they can be tactical, immediate matters, although often there are longer-term knock-on effects. For example, you might be struggling to know what to do about a clash of kids' activities, trying to decide whether to preserve an upcoming day booked off work or debating the next step to take when a work relationship is tricky. It can take up a lot of mental energy trying to think our way out of a situation. Even if we are parking it for later, it's humming away in a circling pattern and nibbling at our reserves of thinking power.

We need quick tools to disrupt the rumination and help us get unstuck. One of the best ways I know how to do this is to map it out. This chapter shares a simple mapping exercise that helps you step back from the detail. Mapping it out in a physical way is very different from keeping it all in your head where it's likely been swirling around for a while.

Drawing on Systems from Chapter 2, we can adapt the approach we learnt about there to look at a current situation and create a map of the mini-system you find yourself in. A simple 3D map of the key things at play in a situation helps you access an external, higher-level view of what's going on. It is then often much easier to see how you can make a move out of the stickiness.

Getting unstuck

We're going to dive right into the activity so that you can get a feel for what we mean by mapping it out. There are a couple of working parent stories that follow this so you can hear how it's helped others get unstuck when they really needed to.

Activity #28: Map it Out[43]

What sticky situation is occupying your mind right now? (e.g. Are you feeling unable to take time off? Might you be unsure how to have a conversation with a colleague? Are you feeling caught between two competing demands?)

- Choose everyday objects around you to be representatives in the map you will make on the table (e.g. a mug, pen, notebook, phone) or use sticky notes to represent the key elements. It can be anything you have to hand. Nobody else will see your map!

[43] Exercise adapted from John Whittington, *Systemic Coaching & Constellations: The Principles, Practices and Application for Individuals, Teams and Groups* (2016), p. 98.

- Place yourself on the map first: choose an object representing you or a sticky note with 'me' written on it. Put it on the table where it feels right.
- Carefully place the other key elements or people on the map one at a time, choosing an object or sticky note to represent each one. Put each element where feels representative in relation to you and to one another. Consider if the items are:
  - Close to you?
  - On top of you?
  - Far away from you?
  - Are other elements close to one another or on opposite sides of the map?
  - Take your time to put them where feels right.
- When you have placed all the most important elements on the map, take a step back. Walk to the other side of the table or sit in a different chair. Get a literal change of perspective.
- Now answer the following questions:
  - What do you notice about your map?
  - If you could capture in a sentence what each element is saying to you, what would that be? (Write it down.)
  - What does that mean for you?
  - If you made one movement on the map that was a step to better, what would that be? Is it even a small turn of direction

for the object representing you to face a different way? Is it a move across the map to somewhere else?

Helicopter view 1

Daniel returned to work after shared parental leave, already aware of his propensity to listen too much to a perfectionist voice and to overplay his strength of dedication to delivery at a high cost to his own wellbeing. He felt anxious, close to 'exploding' at home over small things, and his weekends and bank holidays were being eroded by work.

He had booked a day off at the end of the week to take a break. He was considering cancelling it; at most, he felt 50/50 on his commitment to preserving it but he knew this was not the right answer. What was stopping him from taking a day of leave? He was stuck between competing demands of self, family and deadline pressure at work.

Daniel mapped out the situation on the table. He placed nearby everyday objects to represent the relevant key elements on his map: himself, his wife, his baby, his mother and his work.

- A remote control for the meeting room's a/v system represented 'Work' (the leadership team).
- His wife was represented by a pad of orange sticky notes.
- His son, by a pad of pink sticky notes.
- His Mum was represented by another remote control.
- Daniel was in the middle of all the objects, represented by a pen.

What did he see? He was in the middle of everything and everything was pointing at him. The Work object was almost looming over the top of him, even though the items representing his family were physically more proximate to him. It was interesting to him to see he'd selected remote controls for 'Work' and 'Mum': what was that telling him?

And what were all these different elements and people saying to him?

He challenged his own hypothesis that he was 'not working enough' and could not take a day off. He stepped back and thought carefully. He gave a sentence to summarize what each of the elements on the map were really saying to him:

- Work was saying, 'You have proved yourself, you are doing well, if you were not performing well we would have said so before now'. Furthermore, Work was saying (and he had heard it a few times from people he respected), 'Slow down'.
- His wife was saying, 'Please slow down'.
- His baby son (if he could speak) was saying, 'You are a great Dad. I want to spend time with you; I am only little.'
- His Mum was saying, 'I am proud of you. You are just like me, working so hard, but take a break if you need to.'

Daniel concluded he would be more effective next week if he had time off. He was exhausted. The deadline he had set for himself could wait until next week. It emerged the deadline was not hard and fast for next week even. In fact, it was actually inked in as a deliverable for 3 weeks' time but he had convinced himself that he needed to meet his own early deadline to get ahead and keep up the pace. What had felt like a very difficult decision became an easier call. He took the day off.

Helicopter view 2

Lindsey felt stuck in a difficult work relationship dynamic in the team she led. She was finding it hard to make positive progress with a member of the team and felt she was circling in a draining mode where nothing seemed to improve.

She mapped out the team members on the table, including herself, thinking carefully about where each person should be placed in relation to her and to each other. What became visually clear as she placed sticky notes on the table was how isolated the individual was with whom she was struggling. This person was right on the other side of the map, a long way from Lindsey and the other team members. In fact, the individual looked really lonely.

Lindsey suddenly felt empathy rather than frustration. She reframed what she had initially termed a difficult person to a person who had fallen out of the team boat and was drowning in the water. This individual needed to be pulled back into the boat. Lindsey's forward movement from the circling pattern was to reach out with compassion and make a concerted effort to ensure the individual felt included. If the individual knew she was wanted, her defences would lower and communication might ease. It took some effort but Lindsey reported back that this unlocked a new and much more positive phase of the relationship.

Seeing things from a helicopter perspective in a visual way can release surprising new thoughts, feelings and intentions when we are stuck in the myopia of our own perspective.

Next time you feel stuck, try mapping it out and see what new perspective can be found. Even better, try it with a colleague, friend or partner and ask them to remain quiet while you create the map but then ask you open questions about it when you are ready. For example:

- What are the elements saying to you?
- Which elements feel most difficult to you?
- Which elements are on your side?
- How does it feel to be in this map?
- What do you want to say to yourself as you look at this map?
- What one small move towards better can you make?

Nuggets from Chapter 13

- When you feel stuck with a decision, a situation or a relationship, get a helicopter view to see it afresh. It's easy to feel hemmed in by your own thoughts.
- Create a simple 3D map of the key elements (including you) using everyday objects or sticky notes.
- Place items carefully where it is most right for them to be in the map. Think about proximity to you, others, one another and which direction each element is facing in. Draw arrows on sticky notes if you like.
- Consider one sentence that captures what each element is saying to you. What is one small step towards better in your map? Move a relevant item accordingly.

Part 6

Pulling it all together

'Take the first small steps now towards better.'

(Future You)

14

5 principles and a 'quick tools' guide

In every section of this book, from redefining AC success to prioritization to choosing who to listen to through to getting unstuck, we have been learning new ways of thinking. How you think is at the heart of how you balance the working parent equation in a way that is right for you.

We've covered a lot! I'd like to leave you with a condensed set of principles that are easy to reach for when the pressure is on and which tie everything together. My hope is that these 5 principles will be memorable hooks which connect you back to the detail of what we've covered. There is a 'quick tools' summary under each principle so you can flick straight back to relevant activities.

If you like to have everything in one place with room to scribble, you can download a workbook with all the activities laid out neatly at www.ruddcoaching.co.uk

5 principles for balancing the working parent equation

1. Zoom out
2. Disrupt

3. Communicate
4. Connect
5. Iterate

'Quick tools' guide

1. Zoom out

Step back and see the big picture. Rather than remaining caught in your own myopia or getting stuck in a situation, zoom out and look at things more broadly.

Quick tools:

Seek a future perspective of what is really important: ask 80-year-old you what they see.	Activity #2
In light of 4,000 weeks, what do you want to stop doing? Review your current stop | start | continue.	Activity #3
See the bigger picture of your life: work | family | you. Review the current balance and spot what needs to swap in or out.	Activity #4
Look at how you are more than before and the strengths across the dimensions of your life: what do you bring to work because you are a parent?	Activity #10
Pause and take stock of what you are thankful for. Reflect on what is good right now to switch from the ways you are falling short to what you are grateful for.	Activity #13
Plot the big picture of what you are prioritizing and get ruthless on what you can do, delegate, delete and delay.	Activity #14

What is the balance of the bricks in your Jenga tower? Which bricks need to be swapped around in your stack?	Activity #16
Notice and acknowledge the range of emotions, not just what's negative: look across the full Wheel of Emotions, acknowledge everything you feel and write it down.	Activity #25
Take a helicopter view of problems and issues to get out of the weeds: map out on a table with sticky notes the competing elements at play in your system or situation and see things afresh.	Activity #28

2. Disrupt

Interrupt assumption. Rather than staying caught in the loop of your own thinking or the influence of other people, disrupt unhelpful presumptions, narratives and opinions.

Quick tools:

Disentangle yourself from sticky systems and only take forward what's relevant: say out loud what you are leaving with previous systems and what belongs in the past.	Activity #7
Check the thought that is driving your feelings and behaviour. Rewind the Cognitive Triangle and replace the thought with one that is more balanced and helpful to you.	Activity #8
Mine for alternative perspectives: think like a scientist, historian or journalist and collect evidence to support (or more likely disprove) current thinking.	Activity #9

Spot and categorize guilt. Ask yourself if it is a helpful or harmful sense of guilt by using the Guilt Compass.	Activity #12
Interrupt assumptions you may be making by asking 'how true is that?' Develop some 'catch yourself' questions.	Activity #15
Be ruthless on whose opinions and content you will and won't pay attention to. Ask yourself how helpful these inputs are and put in boundaries around social media, as you would for your child.	Activity #21
Play Thinking Trap Bingo and disrupt the cognitive distortions.	Activity #22
Quieten your inner critic. Use ABCDE to hear what the inner critic is saying to keep you safe and thank it for the warning. Ask yourself 'If I knew the D voice was right, what would I do next?' Pair it with box breathing to get to your most effective thinking.	Activity #23

3. Communicate

Talk with significant others, managers, colleagues and supporters; you don't need to feel alone. Communicate clearly what you need, what you will or will not take on and protect what's most important to you. Employ judicious honesty.

Quick tools:

Consider how you want to communicate about working parenthood at work. What level of honesty would help increase intimacy in the Trust Equation and what honesty will you role-model to the next generation of leaders?	Activity #11

Be prepared to share what's in your 'do' box and communicate to others where you feel overloaded.	Activity #14
Talk about the mental load with your partner and/or others who can support you to categorize and reallocate. Try out 'purple jobs'.	Activity #17
Articulate boundaries and manage expectations: practise politely saying 'no', speaking assertively and not apologizing for having hard lines.	Activity #18

4. Connect

Reconnect to your own purpose, priorities and emotions. Whether you feel isolated and hemmed in or energetic and purposeful, connect with others who can support you in moving forward.

Quick tools:

Reconnect with your BC self: what is important to hold onto in your AC world?	Activity #1
Connect with your 'why': what is important to you about work that makes the balancing act worthwhile?	Activity #5
What might you need to let go of to allow your 'why' to feel valid?	Activity #6
Make a stronger link with your strengths: you are more than before.	Activity #10
Name your inner critic and connect to your 'D' voice. Spend time with this version of yourself: it's a truthful and helpful voice.	Activity #23

Connect to what you are feeling. Acknowledge feelings by saying it's OK and understandable to feel this way and notice what else you are feeling.	Activity #26
Actively meet with your Circle of Support: diarize time to talk with this crucial network to unlock career steps.	Activity #27

5. Iterate

Things don't stand still and a test-and-learn approach keeps us agile. Experiment, reframe 'failing' to 'learning' and discover what works as you, your family and your career evolve.

Quick tools:

Review your non-negotiables as your children grow and your needs change. If something isn't as important as you first thought, consider what the highest value boundaries are now.	Activity #19
Look at grey areas in the prioritization landscape and plot out recent decisions in the three zones. Review and iterate for next time to make different decisions that better reflect your non-negotiables.	Activity #20
Review your engagement in social media. To what extent are your habits supporting a sense of confidence and happiness? You can adopt new habits.	Activity #21
Rediscover the way breathing can shift your physiology, enabling you to iterate your thinking to more balanced and useful inner narratives.	Activity #24

See emotions as data to help you iterate your responses. Use the Wheel of Emotions to test and learn what you are observing in others and feeling internally. Experiment with labelling emotions, acknowledging them, listening to them and responding.	Activity #26
Actively review your Circle of Support: iterate as your career and your needs evolve.	Activity #27

Use the quick tools table and go straight to the bit you need right now!

15

Milky Ways and curve balls

Your Milky Way

That's (almost) it. Kudos for giving yourself the precious time to read this far. I hope you feel equipped with new approaches that help you make good decisions on which parts of your working parent equation need review and focus. I hope you have tools to access liberated, helpful thinking. I hope you feel encouraged by all the voices you've heard and the insights fellow working parents have shared. You are not alone.

As you navigate the delicate act of balancing your small humans and big careers without losing yourself along the way, there is more margin than you realize. You are more in control than you know.

Let's put the myth of 'having it all' to one side and instead pursue the clarity that facilitates having what's really important to you. When you know what your version of success looks like, how to access better-quality thinking, who you will listen to and how to get unstuck, there is so much potential to rebalance the equation your way.

Your mind is your biggest ally; learning how to help it unlock your best thinking is the key to holding those big boulders at bay and creating space for you. Thanks for deciding to spend the time with us.

You deserve to have your Milky Way and eat it!

A few final words: Learning from a big curve ball

As I got to about 80% of the way through writing the draft of this book, I noticed a persistent sensation of pins and needles in my hands and feet. It progressed to numbness, loss of balance and my vision became blurry in one eye.

I went from living a normal working-parent life to an increasing state of physical limitation and a rapid succession of emergency room experiences and invasive medical tests. After a difficult period of uncertainty and confusing and contradictory messages, I was diagnosed with Multiple Sclerosis (MS).

I won't lie. It felt like a hammer blow. A huge shock. There was an enormous amount to process emotionally and physically. It felt like we'd dropped into a parallel universe. To say my family and I felt overwhelmed is an understatement.

Diagnosis was the end of the beginning. It became clear this was not a case of getting through a tough period of ill health in order to reach a hoped-for state of recovery. It would be about learning to live with a lifelong condition. MS is a chronic degenerative neurological condition for which there is no cure. Disability in difficult, limiting and humiliating ways can be the experience for many people with MS. You can imagine what was going through our heads.

The uncertainty of the future was, and remains, hard to deal with as we tried to get our heads around the impact on our family life first and foremost. We gratefully leant on family, friends and our faith. I put work to one side and reassured myself that there would be a time to pick this back up again in the future.

If you also have dealt with serious health news in your family, you will know the rollercoaster all too well. You may be facing into something more challenging than we are. You may understand the pain of wanting to tell your family it will all be OK but knowing instead that they will all need to adjust, like you. You will feel grief for the future you thought you might enjoy and the knock-on for others you care about. And yet, you all grow in resilience and find a way through.

I would like to share some final thoughts, sharpened by this personal experience, that may be helpful as you consider how radically or how swiftly you wish to review your own working parent equation.

The time is now

Maybe you've caught yourself thinking, 'I'll take a look at all this when I have a bit more time'. Well, speaking frankly, that's a gamble.

I am so glad I made changes a few years ago that enabled me to spend time on the things I most wanted and needed to. Even still, I have regrets for the activities we said we'd do another year, the adventures we thought could wait and the times I was so busy that I overlooked the importance of health. With innovations in medication, a lot more may be possible but it's not guaranteed.

80-year-old me looks rather different from the version I met up with in the past. 4,000 weeks is not a guarantee and neither is how well and able we will be for whatever number of weeks we are given.

As I listen to working parents wrestling with ways to carve out enough time to see their children in the week, being burdened with self-doubt or fearing that shifting gears for a few months will stall their careers, I wish, with your permission, to share my reflections:

- You will not regret taking the balance across work | family | you seriously now (and I mean right now).
- You have everything to gain by taming the inner critic who holds you back from allowing yourself to prioritize what's in your heart and what makes you sustainably healthy.
- You can change the way you feel and behave for the better by getting to more true and helpful thinking and you can be a lot more present now, not at some future date.

Your health is a non-negotiable

There is so much research and science that supports the need for every one of us to prioritize holistic health and wellbeing.

It simply cannot loiter at the bottom of a to-do list. When much about MS seemed out of my control, it helped to learn there were things I could influence through the way I looked after myself. And the benefits are not limited to managing a condition.

Prevention is always better than a cure. Our levels of stress, our diet, exercise and exposure to daylight play a significant part in prevention of and recovery from many modern lifestyle diseases, such as cancer, heart disease, type 2 diabetes, autoimmune disorders, and the list goes on. Interestingly, sunlight (Vitamin D), Omega-3, stress relief and a diet low in saturated fat are particularly important for those with MS.[44]

I've made some significant shifts to diet, supplements, exercise, stress relief and time outside. I reflect that if I were not living with MS, I would now be feeling absolutely amazing most of the time! The mind-body connection is real and it is vital. Whether you are dealing with illness or sailing close to the wind on burnout, stress and anxiety, it's a fact that learning to improve your mind and how it works does impact the brain and therefore every cell in your body (i.e. your physical health). Thoughts are not imaginary or illusory; neuroscience has shown us they form proteins in the brain. And this directly impacts your body, such as the level of inflammation, your immune system, your organs and your nervous system.

My hope in sharing this personal perspective is that you step back and view your mind and body as miraculous

[44] Professor George Jelenik's book, *Overcoming Multiple Sclerosis*, 2016, is a research-based, practical and optimistic book. It puts forward a compelling case for lifestyle changes in conjunction with medication that can lead to significantly better outcomes for people with MS all around the world.

and deserving of good care. Your amazing being is reliant on you making good decisions on what you put into your body, what you allow into your thinking, how you move, how much you feel the sunlight on your skin and how you nurture your soul.

Waiting until next week, next month or next year to take your health and wellbeing seriously is a poor bet. We're back to 'the time is now'.

Appreciate today

Whilst I can't say that I am thankful for MS, there is inevitably good that emerges from difficulty. Living with something long term requires a determination to live more in the present. Each day is a day to be thankful for, if we are willing to acknowledge it.

I am still the parent, spouse, friend and coach that I was. In some ways I'm an improved version. It's still early days and at some moments it all feels a lot but these are beginning to be the minority of days.

I am thankful for:

- Being stopped in my tracks with a 'busy-doing' approach to life.
- A clearer focus on what really matters to me.
- An even closer relationship with my husband.
- Non-negotiable ordinary time every day with my children (forget #makingmemories on social media).
- Deeper faith and increased gratitude for each new day.

- Vulnerability (intimacy) in friendships which has turbocharged our Trust Equation.
- A continued love for my work.
- Treating my body with greater respect.

It's a joy to rediscover how my version of the Milky Way, the things I most need, are of course what Future Me already knew I should spend my time on. My work is of huge importance and I am thankful to be able to continue to build the career I love. It's firmly in the knowledge that balance with family and wellbeing is non-negotiable. My working parent equation is a 'now' priority. It can't wait for me to find a window in my schedule.

So, what most needs to change in your equation?

Don't wait to claim the margin that's already there. Take the first small steps now towards better. Consider doing less and being more.

Future You is banking on it.

About the author

Georgie Rudd is executive coach of choice for leaders across sectors ranging from financial services to management consulting to retail to Formula 1. A 20-year corporate leadership career with Lloyds Banking Group and as global Head of Learning at Baringa Partners equipped Georgie with the experience, insight and expertise that her clients prize so highly. She understands the challenges of balancing small humans and big careers in demanding high-performance organizations. She knows what it takes to lead in a sustainable way and how to turn development insight into positive action.

Georgie founded Rudd Coaching Ltd in 2020. She is an accredited Professional Certified Coach through the International Coaching Federation, specializing in leadership coaching and working-parent coaching on a one-to-one and group basis. She has coached hundreds of professionals worldwide. Regarded as warm, challenging and incisive, Georgie's clients consider her to be an invaluable thinking partner who elicits the critical things that improve effectiveness, performance, balance and joy.

If you'd like to find out more, why not take a look at further useful resources, training programmes, coaching programmes and speaking opportunities at www.ruddcoaching.co.uk

Acknowledgements

I always enjoy reading about the people who stand behind a book I've spent time with. There are literally hundreds of people to thank for this book coming into being: every client generously creates and shares new learning and a fresh perspective.

Those who kindly allowed me to share their experiences and reflections with you deserve a special mention. The honest and likeable voices you hear in *The Working Parent Equation* are the stars of the show. I won't name them as they may not appreciate such transparency! However, you know who you are. A heartfelt thank you.

There are too many friends to mention but particular thanks to these special people whose love, loyalty and practical support have helped us through the hardest of times: Roz S., Linz H., Fi L., Elizabeth T., Caroline C., Sal B., Hannah N., Becky L.-B., Heather F., Tim C., Helen C., Sarah M., Penny F. and Jen W. You embody the Trust Equation.

Thank you to Nina J. who helps us balance our working parent equation with characteristic humour, care and commitment: you are so appreciated.

Thank you to my husband, Ben, who never doubts my ability (he's my 'D voice' personified) and is my loving team-mate as we strive to balance our equation. In recent times, he's had to hold more than before in every way and I am so grateful for his kindness, love of fun, logic, optimism and generosity of spirit.

To our brilliant girls, it is our privilege to be your parents. You inspire us daily, you make us laugh out loud and you are growing up to be young women of noble character. Thanks for letting me share some of your superb insights and scribblings.

Thank you to Rachel Burnham for her humorous and apposite illustrations. Thank you to the Practical Inspiration Publishing authors for your camaraderie and input. Thanks also to those people who read early drafts and gave me honest feedback. And a big thanks to Alison Jones and the whole Practical Inspiration Publishing team in progressing this from an idea to a fully-fledged book.

Finally, thank you to my parents, Paul and Diana. It is only now that I am a parent that I fully appreciate the balancing act you pulled off so skilfully. I am grateful for the strong family values, love, supportiveness and belief that defines the family system I grew up in. I take these forward gladly. I admire and applaud your ability to love through the good and the hard times in life… and to let go, which increasingly emerges as a key parenting skill. I'm still learning from you: parenting is for life, not just the first 18 years!

Thanks to you for reading this book. Why not pass it on? We're all in this together.

References

Benson, Kyle. *The Magic Relationship Ratio, According to Science*. The Gottman Institute (2024). Available from: www.gottman.com/blog/the-magic-relationship-ratio-according-science/ [accessed 24 March 2025].

Brown, Brené. *I Thought It Was Just Me (but It Isn't): Making the Journey from 'What Will People Think?' to 'I Am Enough'* (2007).

Brown, Brené. *Dare to Lead: Brave Work. Tough Conversations. Whole Hearts* (2018).

Burkeman, Oliver. *Four Thousand Weeks: Time Management for Mortals* (2022).

Clance, Pauline Rose and Imes, Suzanne. 'The Imposter Phenomenon in High Achieving Women: Dynamics and Therapeutic Intervention', in *Psychotherapy Theory, Research and Practice*, 15 (3), 241–7 (1978).

Covey, Stephen R. *The 7 Habits of Highly Effective People* (1989).

David, Susan. *Recognizing Your Emotions as Data, Not Directives* (2022). Available from: www.susandavid.com/newsletter/recognizing-your-emotions-as-data-not-directives/ [accessed 1 March 2024].

Fisher, Jefferson. *The Speaking Coach: The One Word All Liars Use! Stop Saying This Word, It's Making You Sound Weak! The More You Do This, The More You Sound Like a Liar*, The Diary of a CEO with Steven Bartlett (2025). Available from: https://podcasts.apple.com/gb/podcast/the-diary-of-a-ceo-with-steven-bartlett/id1291423644?i=1000699457581 [accessed 24 November 2025].

Gervais, Michael. *The First Rule of Mastery: Stop Worrying about What People Think of You* (2023).

Goldsmith, Marshall. *What Got You Here Won't Get You There: How Successful People Become Even More Successful* (2008).

Goleman, Daniel. *Emotional Intelligence: Why It Can Matter More Than IQ* (1996).

Grant, Adam. *Think Again: The Power of Knowing What You Don't Know* (2021).

Haidt, Jonathan. *The Anxious Generation: How the Great Rewiring of Childhood Is Causing an Epidemic of Mental Illness* (2025).

Hamilton, Chloe. *'I Feel Like I'm on Holiday!': Inside Our Week-Long Mental Load Marriage Swap*. The Guardian (2025). Available from: www.theguardian.com/lifeandstyle/2025/mar/05/i-feel-like-im-on-holiday-inside-our-week-long-mental-load-marriage-swap [accessed 15 April 2025].

Hogenboom, Melissa. *The Hidden Load: How Thinking of Everything Holds Mums Back*. BBC (2021). Available from: www.bbc.co.uk/worklife/article/20210518-the-hidden-load-how-thinking-of-everything-holds-mums-back [accessed 19 January 2025].

Hugh, Carol. *How Working Parents Can Strategically Prioritize Their Time* Harvard Business Review (2021). Available from: www.hbr.org/2021/04/how-working-parents-can-strategically-prioritize-their-time [accessed 30 September 2024].

Jelenik, George. *Overcoming Multiple Sclerosis: The Evidence Based 7-Step Recovery Programme* (2016).

Kaplowitz, Lisa S. and Mangino, Kate. *Research: Caregiver Employees Bring Unique Value to Companies. Harvard Business Review* (2023). Available from: www.hbr.org/2023/08/research-caregiver-employees-bring-unique-value-to-companies [accessed 12 March 2025].

Kline, Nancy. *Time to Think: Listening to Ignite the Human Mind* (1999).

Maister, David H., Green, Charles H. and Galford, Robert M. *The Trusted Advisor* (2001).

Neff, Kristin. *Self-Compassion: Stop Beating Yourself Up and Leave Insecurity Behind* (2011).

Pareto's 80-20 Rule Theory Business Balls (n.d.) Available from: www.businessballs.com/planning-workload-time-management-and-prioritisation/pareto-80-20-rule-theory/ [accessed 20 November 2025].

Pederson, Traci. *Too Many Extracurricular Activities for Kids May Do More Harm Than Good.* PsychCentral (2018). Available from: www.psychcentral.com/news/2018/05/15/too-many-extracurricular-activities-for-kids-may-do-more-harm-than-good#1 [accessed 14 December 2024].

Robinson, Lawrence. *Social Media and Mental Health: Are you Addicted to Social Media?* HelpGuide (2025). Available from: www.helpguide.org/mental-health/wellbeing/social-media-and-mental-health [accessed 8 September 2025].

The 8 Key Leadership Skills You Need to Know in 2025. International Management Development Institute (2025). Available from: www.imd.org/blog/leadership/leadership-skills/ [accessed 20 November 2025].

The Feelings Wheel: Unlock the Power of Your Emotions. Calm (2025). Available from: www.calm.com/blog/the-feelings-wheel [accessed 20 November 2025].

Tupper, Helen and Ellis, Sarah. *The Squiggly Career: Ditch the Ladder, Discover Opportunity, Design Your Career* (2024).

Whittington, John. *Systemic Coaching & Constellations: The Principles, Practices and Application for Individuals, Teams and Groups* (2nd edition, 2016).

Index

www.ingramcontent.com/pod-product-compliance
Lightning Source LLC
Chambersburg PA
CBHW032151080426
42735CB00008B/668

* 9 7 8 1 7 8 8 6 0 8 7 3 2 *